Taking THE Reins

INSIGHTS INTO THE WORLD OF

ULTRA-WEALTHY

INHERITORS

Russ Alan Prince   **Jared Dubey**
Richard J. Flynn   **Brett Van Bortel**

Charter Financial Publishing Network
499 Broad Street, Suite 120
Shrewsbury, NJ 07702

Taking the Reins: Insights Into the World of Ultra-Wealthy Inheritors
By Russ Alan Prince, Jared Dubey, Richard J. Flynn, Brett Van Bortel

Design: Martine Cameau | cameaudesign.com

ISBN-13: 978-0-9766574-7-7

TO JERRY, ALL MY LOVE
(REMEMBER: AN UNFUNDED TRUST FUND DOESN'T MEAN YOU'RE RICH)

Russ Alan Prince

TO MY FAMILY

Jared Dubey

TO MOM AND DAD, THANK YOU FOR YOUR LOVE AND FOR ALWAYS BEING SUPPORTIVE TO ALL OF US. ENJOY!

Richard J. Flynn

TO NICK, JAKE AND CATERINA,
"TO THOSE WHO MUCH IS GIVEN MUCH IS REQUIRED"

Brett Van Bortel

TABLE OF CONTENTS

FOREWORD

by Carl L. Liederman

AS A LONG-STANDING TRUSTED LEGAL ADVISOR

to many ultra-high-net-worth individuals and family offices, I was delighted to see that the findings of *Taking the Reins* reflected my personal experience and reinforced my belief that this generation of ultra-wealthy inheritors is truly extraordinary and unique. They are the most connected, committed, and considered (in their analysis and focus on meaningful impact) generation of inheritors in living memory, across all countries and sectors. They are global citizens in the best sense of the term, less interested in nationality, and more focused on understanding and then solving the world's most pressing issues on an international scale.

Taking the Reins provides insights into the world of ultra-wealthy inheritors based on a sample population of 114, with 71 of those working in their family's single-family office (SFO). A large proportion (41.2%) of the respondents identify their home base as "North America." Some may argue that this predominance may undermine the overall relevance of the findings. I disagree. I have worked with, mentored, fundraised, and advised the target population throughout the world. Based on my experience, I would recommend that the reader minimize the inherent limitations of the study and focus on the findings for I can attest, without reservation, that the issues identified apply to every ultra-high-net-worth inheritor I know.

For me, the most compelling findings are as follows. First, the most probable cause of "downfall" for an inheritor is lack of knowledge and attention. This means that inheritors must be informed, educated and plugged into the right peer groups, advisors, and networks. Since 88.6% of those surveyed want to do something significant in the world, the knowledge they seek must be global in scope. Interestingly, 97.2% of SFO respondents and 76.7% of individual respondents participated in "conclaves," but there is a danger that these enclaves can be self-reinforcing. It is difficult to change the world if you only see it largely through one lens. To borrow a term from the book, this is a generation of "knowledge entrepreneurs" and knowledge transcends socio-economic boundaries.

As someone who has served in many leadership positions at law firms and global charities, I found myself nodding vigorously when reading the study's findings on the key attributes of professionals in *Chapter 9: Selecting Professional Advisors*. These attributes include transparency, no hidden agenda, open and regular communications, and full disclosure. The fact is that the world has changed. There are no secrets. People expect transparency and can quickly name-and-shame through social media. They expect and demand full accountability from their advisors, institutions, and those charities they choose to support.

In this context, the choice of advisors becomes paramount, especially for ultra-wealthy inheritors. They have the greatest power and thus the most to lose. In this context, *Taking the Reins* highlights the importance of finding, securing, and maintaining a network of trusted global advisors who can address the myriad and complex needs of ultra-wealthy inheritors. With the right advisors, this generation can quite literally transform the world for the better.

I know and respect Jared Dubey and congratulate him and Russ Alan Prince, Richard J. Flynn, and Brett Van Bortel for this valuable, informative, and timely study. They have identified and highlighted the key issues for these inheritors and, by doing so, have shown their commitment, desire, and aptitude to be the global advisors of choice for the next generation.

Carl L. Liederman
Trusted Advisor to Family Offices and Foundations

ABOUT THIS BOOK

There's wealthy, and then there's ultra-wealthy. We define ultra-wealthy as having a net worth of US$100 million or more for individuals, or controlling US$500 million or more in a single-family office structure. Our aim in this treatise is to provide a rare empirically based view of a very select segment of the magnificently affluent: the current and future inheritors of Brobdingnagian fortunes, many of whom are taking steps to create wealth in their own right as well as productively changing the world.

The reason for conducting this research endeavor, resulting is this exposition and the accompanying educational programs, are the ultra-wealthy inheritors themselves. In working with them in our respective professional capacities, they've been very clear in wanting to know:

- How ultra-wealthy inheritors are successfully dealing with similar issues and concerns. While all situations are indeed different, there are likenesses, and the way other ultra-wealthy inheritors deal with these matters and the results they attain is of extreme interest to them.

- How ultra-wealthy inheritors are effectively navigating the world while managing their affluence and obligations. They're particularly focused on the ways they can make a meaningful difference.

- How ultra-wealthy inheritors could potentially be more productive and effectual in their own lives through a broader and deeper understanding of the options available to them. Included here is the ability to grow their wealth and their interest in deal making.

- How ultra-wealthy inheritors can enhance and better focus their abilities to more efficaciously achieve their agendas. Ultra-wealthy inheritors, for example, tend to have very powerful and extensive networks. Many of them are not effectively leveraging their networks nearly as well as they potentially can.

Taking the Reins is not a journalistic account or a set of profiles knitted together. It's not a historical exposition of great wealth, nor does the book have a political orientation. It's neither a celebration nor a critique of great wealth. At the same time, it's not a manifesto of the benefits and disadvantages of coming into a substantial inheritance or being a member of an exceptionally affluent family. This treatise is not about how society should be or what ultra-wealthy inheritors should do or not do with their monies or their lives. Instead, we're examining and analyzing what these ultra-wealthy inheritors are currently doing and, in some scenarios, intend to do.

We were tasked with developing a more refined and better understanding of certain issues, potentials, and key decisions of a growing significant and extraordinarily influential cohort. Ultra-wealthy inheritors have the potential to make a dramatic positive impact on select aspects of our world. We've found that many of them are ardently seeking ways to maximize that potential.

We surveyed 43 individual ultra-wealthy inheritors and 71 ultra-wealthy inheritors working in their family's single-family offices on an array of topics, some of which we deal with herein. We readily recognize and admit to the manifold limitations of this research program. Included here is the inability to broadly generalize from our conclusions (see *Appendix: Limitations When Researching Wealth*). Having for decades extensively studied professionals in the service of the wealthy and expansively studied the wealthy per se—including the ultra-wealthy—we're quite familiar with the optimal ways to appreciate, interpret, and use the research findings and implications. We're also keenly aware of the many and diverse restrictions of the results.

A very important consideration is that we're looking at a very unique group of creative, caring, open-minded, and opportunistic individuals at one moment in time. Their vast wealth often enables a great many of them to—relatively quickly—readjust to changing and consequential circumstances. This means that the detections and insights conveyed in these pages are likely to match, potentially quickly and sometimes dramatically, evolving circumstances.

With these significant caveats in place, what we've found is how ultra-wealthy inheritors are presently addressing a number of crucial financial, societal, and personal matters. We chose to focus on some of the more informative findings such as:

- Their overarching approach to some of their philanthropic activities.

- The issues concerning the financial management of their fortunes.

- How they're dealing with select pressing and often-ubiquitous concerns.

What's evident is that ultra-wealthy inheritors have or are incrementally *taking the reins* from previous generations. In our sample, they have or are in the process of determining their own paths both in business and philanthropy. This doesn't mean they're not actively involved with their families, but they're striking off on their own in a multitude of ways or are intimately involved in setting the direction for their families.

This book and its companion educational programs provide possible ways for ultra-wealthy inheritors to become more effectual in actualizing their goals and objectives. The material herein may also provide viable and evocative lessons and perspectives for those less financially endowed.

PART I

Dynastic Wealth

ULTRA-WEALTHY
INHERITORS

A FINANCIAL DYNASTY can be defined as a family who maintains its important economic position across generations. By transferring serious and considerable monies to the next generation and potentially further down the familial line, we have a financial family dynasty.

What often happens in financial family dynasties is a transformation in the way in which these monies are applied. Even in situations where the monies are "locked" due to trusts or are being pooled and overseen as in the case of a single-family office, there's usually a clear evolution in thinking and action that causes a divergence from previous generations. What we find very much in evidence in the current transformation is the considerable intensity with which the ultra-wealthy inheritors are taking and looking to take control of their lives and finances with clear broad aims in mind.

For this research project, we developed two samples of ultra-wealthy inheritors with overlapping definitions. **Individual ultra-wealthy inheritors** meet the following two criteria:

CRITERION #1 **The family fortune was initially amassed by a member of a previous generation.** While there have been individuals who took comparatively modest inheritances and transformed them into great wealth, our focus is on those ultra-wealthy inheritors who were bequeathed great wealth. As we'll see, the affluence of some of the inheritors we surveyed goes back a few generations.

CRITERION #2 **The respondent has risen to a position responsible—to some degree—for a personal or familial fortune worth US$100 million or more.** The individual answering the survey is a major contributing decision-maker for a sizable fortune we define as US$100 million or more. Moreover, he or she will have inherited the monies or is expecting to do so.

Due to the nature of family relationships, ofttimes coupled with the way the wealth is structured, there are many situations where ownership and control over the assets are divergent or constrained. In addition, the precise level of influence in financial and related decisions of the respondent was independently impossible to ascertain. Consequently, we've chosen to err in the direction of "major contributing decision-maker."

For ultra-wealthy inheritors working in their families' single-family offices (referred to throughout the manuscript as **SFO ultra-wealthy inheritors**), the following criteria were used:

CRITERION #1 **The family fortune was initially amassed by a member of a previous generation.** This is the same as for individual ultra-wealthy inheritors. It was the wealth creator or another family member from a previous generation who created the wealth, which underpins the single-family office where the survey respondent is employed.

CRITERION #2 **The respondent has a senior leadership position in their family's single-family office that controls US$500 million or more.** The individuals answering the survey are decision-makers—senior executives, if not the executive directors—at their respective single-family offices. Moreover, the single-family offices are stand-along entities directing a substantial pool of investable assets and may also be involved in the operational issues of ongoing family enterprises.

CRITERION #3 **The respondent has or expects to directly inherit US$100 million or more.** The single-family office might still manage or oversee these monies. Nevertheless, the ultra-wealthy inheritor now or in the future will have ownership and control over of these funds.

BUILDING A SAMPLE OF ULTRA-WEALTHY INHERITORS

There are a plethora of issues and complications—serious limitations—when empirically studying the wealthy. These matters are exponentially complicated as we go up the wealth spectrum making surveying and interviewing the ultra-wealthy a complex, periodically convoluted, and regularly arduous venture replete with undeterminable imprecision. There are also a slew of methodological issues and considerations when researching single-family offices. We recognize the various complications of researching this elite cohort (see *Appendix: Limitations When Researching Wealth*). Nevertheless, by tapping into strong discerning personal and professional/institutional networks, we were able to construct a sample of 114 ultra-wealthy inheritors as we've defined them (see above).

Just to put this sample into perspective, according to Wealth-X, a global ultra-high-net-worth prospecting, intelligence, and wealth due diligence firm, across the globe there are 52,625 families worth US$100 million or more controlling US$19.545 trillion (Exhibit 1.1). Furthermore, Wealth-X forecasts a 6.2% average annual growth rate for the ultra-wealthy from 2013 to 2018.

EXHIBIT 1.1 The Ultra-Wealthy

Number of families	**52,625**
Aggregate assets	**US$19.545 trillion**

Source: Wealth-X, 2013

What's very telling is that there aren't any viable estimates of the number of ultra-wealthy inheritors or the monies they personally control or influence. While there's considerable private wealth industry consensus that these inheritors are playing an increasingly important role, and they constitute a rapidly expanding cohort, any assessments of their numbers and aggregate assets they own or control are limited to informed guesses.

A related complication is that there's no definitive assessment of the number of single-family offices. Since these are often bespoke financial and supportive organizations dedicated to the ofttimes idiosyncratic needs and preferences of an exceptionally affluent family, even coming up with a consensus definition of a single-family office can be problematic.

Another point we want to emphasize here is that by employing chain-referral sampling, we've built a sample of ultra-wealthy inheritors who likely have a more similar than dissimilar mind-set. For instance, many strongly expressed having family responsibilities and obligations meaning they are not voluptuaries relishing all the pleasures and amusements that money can buy (see *Chapter 3: With Great Wealth Comes Great Responsibility*). Moreover, by working between and through "hubs" of single-family offices, we've potentially biased the sample because of their similar interests and concerns.

An overall characteristic of this cohort, for example, is their drive to achieve (see *Chapter 3: With Great Wealth Comes Great Responsibility*). While many of them will likely have different agendas, there's the overall pervasive "want" to accomplish. This is especially evident, for example, in their generally pronounced strong interest in taking the reins.

Another common quality of many of the ultra-wealthy inheritors we researched is their commitment to philanthropy (see *Chapter 5: Philanthropy*). While this takes various forms including impact investing (see *Chapter 6: Wealth Management*), many of the research participants clearly want to take actions that can change the world or some corner of it for the better.

At this moment in time. For ultra-wealthy inheritors, as well as those interested in them, there's another major complication and drawback to the research findings. There are many indications that the economic, social, and political environments the ultra-wealthy inheritors are living in today are quickly evolving. This, of course, is also true of those less financially endowed, but the implications are likely to be very different.

The technological revolution we're now living through, for example, is transforming the work world and society while creating new vast fortunes. From innovative Internet-based businesses and products to the transformation of manufacturing with the likes of 3-D printing, new technologies will change all our lives. The result will be vast new fortunes as well as opportunities to dramatically expand existing fortunes.

With high-quality and specialized information becoming ever more ubiquitous, easily accessible and—very importantly—free, many industries from traditional media to traditional education are going to have to reinvent themselves or they'll likely fade away. Consequently, thought leaders will dominate and accrue the greater percentage of the corporate, and consequently, the greatest percentage of personal riches. Whether it's professional services or luxury marketing or leveraging sales through search engine optimization, the recognized authorities will dominate in our "winner-take-most" entrepreneurial capitalistic milieu. There are only going to be a relatively small number of thought leaders, and they're going to also create astounding personal fortunes.

Another glaring example is the marriage of technology and healthcare. For example, while certain concierge medical practices (see *Chapter 17: Connected Care for the High-Net-Worth Family: Millennials Will Lead the Way*) are bringing cutting-edge technology supported by a hyper-responsive medical service model to the treatment of wealthy clients in transit, these practices will soon be made increasingly available to everyone. It's just that, presently, the very affluent are the ones financing the development of these integrated methodologies. A number of the individuals leading these initiatives will create sizeable fortunes as well.

What does this mean for the research results cited herein? As it's quite evident that many ultra-wealthy inheritors are exceptionally astute, flexible, and shrewd, they will not only readily adjust to these changes, it's expected that a percentage of them will likely be at the forefront. Accordingly, the research findings sited in this treatise will in short order require updating. It's highly probabilistic that as ultra-wealthy inheritors adapt and foster these changes, their answers to many of the survey questions will unquestionably change.

All told, this sample of 114 ultra-wealthy inheritors is absolutely NOT representative of all ultra-wealthy inheritors. At best, the results characterize this particular set of individuals at this moment in time. The results do provide direction and should serve as a basis for further research. The findings, moreover, can prove useful enabling ultra-wealthy inheritors to start making personal and professional comparisons as well as more informed decisions. The research results can also be insightful for professional advisors working with, or wanting to work with, this elite cohort.

With these robust disclaimers in place, we now turn to the demographics of our sample.

ROLL CALL

By design, there are two types of ultra-wealthy inheritors we surveyed—individuals and those working in their families' single-family offices. In total, 114 ultra-wealthy inheritors completed the survey instrument. The majority of them are SFO ultra-wealthy inheritors (Exhibit 1.2).

EXHIBIT 1.2

Segmentation Model

N = 114 ultra-wealthy inheritors

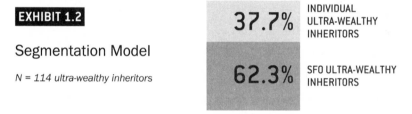

37.7% INDIVIDUAL ULTRA-WEALTHY INHERITORS

62.3% SFO ULTRA-WEALTHY INHERITORS

Seven out of ten of the ultra-wealthy inheritors were male (Exhibit 1.3). However, among the individual ultra-wealthy inheritors, 56% were female. Meanwhile, a large majority (85%) of the SFO ultra-wealthy inheritors are male. The fact that male family members are more highly represented in their single-family offices mirrors the financial services industry in general.

EXHIBIT 1.3 Gender

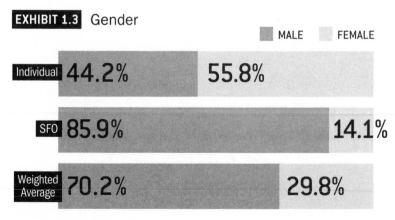

MALE FEMALE

Individual 44.2% 55.8%
SFO 85.9% 14.1%
Weighted Average 70.2% 29.8%

N = 114 ultra-wealthy inheritors

The majority of the ultra-wealthy inheritors are between 30 and 40 years old (Exhibit 1.4). Half the individual ultra-wealthy inheritors are in this age range compared to only a third of the SFO ultra-wealthy inheritors.

EXHIBIT 1.4 Age

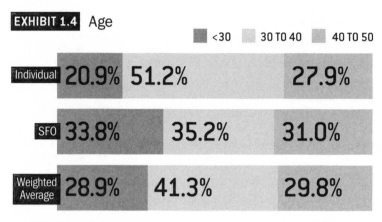

N = 114 ultra-wealthy inheritors

By definition, the sample is composed of people who were not the original wealth creators (Exhibit 1.5). About two-fifths of the ultra-wealthy inheritors are second generation. This is strongly influenced by the family members working in their single-family offices. Meanwhile, the individual ultra-wealthy inheritors tend to be third generation or greater.

EXHIBIT 1.5 Generation

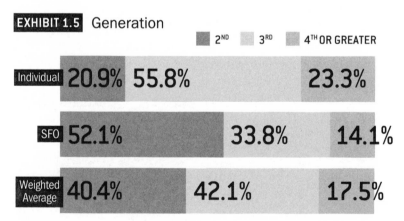

N = 114 ultra-wealthy inheritors

The second generation is the one where the individual ultra-wealthy inheritors have the highest probability of being immersed in a life devoid of great monies. The wealth creator, for instance, could have been building a great company that didn't produce the family fortune until it was sold. Thus, his or her children were possibly growing up without a great deal of discretionary monies. In contrast, past the second generation, the family fortune exists as they were growing up. The access and influence a third or later generation family member would have is now more exclusively a function of family dynamics.

With respect to family members working in their families' single-family offices, by the nature of family offices, the wealth creators have amassed substantial investable assets needing professional management. Many types of generational differences become less decisive in these situations.

About three-quarters of the ultra-wealthy inheritors identify themselves as being in a meaningful relationship (Exhibit 1.6). The remainder of the sample doesn't. Having a partner—broadly defined—can potentially have consequential implications when it comes to effective financial and legal planning.

EXHIBIT 1.6 Personal Relationship

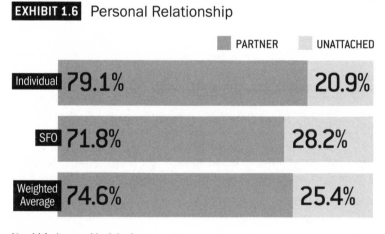

N = 114 ultra-wealthy inheritors

While the sample is clearly limited, it's important to note that it's international in nature (Exhibit 1.7). Two-fifths are from North America. Three out of ten define themselves as being transnational with SFO ultra-wealthy inheritors weighing in more heavily. This is represented in a number of scenarios. The two most common are where the ultra-wealthy inheritors have multiple citizenships or where they have a single citizenship, but live widely throughout the world thereby not identifying exclusively with a single country or region.

EXHIBIT 1.7 Home Base

LOCATION	INDIVIDUAL	SFO	WEIGHTED AVERAGE
North America	41.9%	40.8%	41.2%
Transnational	20.9%	36.6%	30.7%
Europe	16.3%	16.9%	16.7%
South America	9.3%	1.5%	4.4%
Middle East	4.6%	2.8%	3.5%
Asia/Far East	7.0%	1.4%	3.5%

N = 114 ultra-wealthy inheritors

Because of the diverse places many of the ultra-wealthy call home, it's not surprising that about half report traveling extensively with 60% SFO ultra-wealthy inheritors doing so (Exhibit 1.8). About 30% say they travel periodically, with a sixth reporting they travel very little. These lifestyles highlight the common need for ready access to high quality medical and family security resources (see *Chapter 8: Critical Lifestyle Services; Chapter 17: Connected Care for the High-Net-Worth Family: Millennials Will Lead the Way; Chapter 18: Combating Professional Criminals; Chapter 19: Taking Matters Into Their Own Hands*).

As the sample is international in nature coupled with a tendency for many of them to travel extensively, we find that we're regularly dealing with truly global citizens. While many have psychological ties to particular geographies and countries, these ties are not always especially strong. This helps set the stage for them to become global stewards (see *Chapter 11: The Education of Global Stewards*).

A substantial number of them think in terms of the world as opposed to a more limited topography. This mightily impacts how they approach their personal and financial lives. Never before in history has there been greater ease of mobility in terms of people and capital. This worldview dramatically impacts all aspects of their decision-making from which philanthropic causes to support to where to invest.

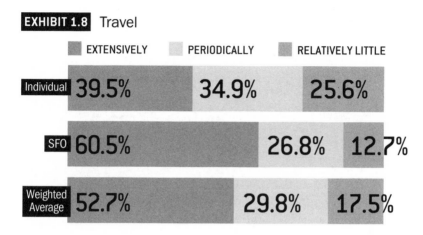

EXHIBIT 1.8   Travel

N = 114 ultra-wealthy inheritors

From a look at the demographics, there's clearly a fair amount of diversity in the sample. Still, what singularly best defines this cohort is the monies they've inherited and, in some cases, the family wealth they influence. That's not to say that many of them haven't engaged in business dealings that magnified their fortunes, but the foundation of their wealth was—to date—passed down to them. That said, the question becomes the source of their wealth.

DRIVERS OF WEALTH

Nearly all great wealth can trace its origins back to highly successful private enterprises. The successes of these endeavors translate into significant family monies. Sometimes the businesses remain in the hands of the family over the generations. At other times, the businesses are monetized providing capital for other business endeavors and investment activities. However, the question is what is driving wealth maintenance or creation today.

With respect to the ultra-wealthy inheritors surveyed, the answer is their investment portfolios—a function of the SFO ultra-wealthy inheritors in the sample (Exhibit 1.9). For about two-thirds—mostly individual ultra-wealthy inheritors—currently operating family businesses are creating their wealth. A number of the survey respondents are part of family founded and managed conglomerates. Others are immersed in singular highly successful family enterprises.

For a third—again principally individual ultra-wealthy inheritors—non-family businesses are drivers of their fortunes.

EXHIBIT 1.9 Major Driver of Family/Personal Wealth

DRIVERS	INDIVIDUAL	SFO	WEIGHTED AVERAGE
Investment portfolio	23.3%	95.8%	68.4%
Family business	72.1%	57.7%	63.2%
Non-family business	55.8%	19.7%	33.3%

N = 114 ultra-wealthy inheritors

It's critical to understand that ultra-wealthy inheritors are generally very different than significant wealth creators. This proves to usually be the case even as some of these ultra-wealthy inheritors create ever-greater personal fortunes.

ALL THE ULTRA-WEALTHY ARE THE SAME, EXCEPT WHEN THEY'RE NOT

From experience, through the findings of decades of research and working closely with the ultra-wealthy, what we've always found quite telling is that there are frequently meaningful and weighty differences among various segments based on how they became so affluent. To provide a better understanding of the differences, we compare the self-made ultra-wealthy with ultra-wealthy inheritors on a number of criteria (Exhibit 1.10).

What's important to bear in mind is that we're taking a very broad-based view, which produces degrees of inaccuracy. Precision in these matters is impossible, while it's surely possible to get a "feel" for the differences.

Wealth creation. For the self-made ultra-wealthy, wealth creation is often central and critical to their very identities. A person will rarely amass such a Croesus fortune unless he or she is intensely committed to becoming extraordinarily affluent. The extreme motivation for building such a large personal fortune is regularly the very incentive to do so— what we refer to as the *wealth creation high*.

For ultra-wealthy inheritors, greater wealth creation might be a major concern. However, it's rarely given the near exclusive intense emphasis that the self-made ultra-wealthy tend to give it. The personal and professional agendas of ultra-wealthy inheritors are regularly quite different, usually more expansive, often leading to lesser weight placed on personal wealth creation.

Family. Creating a momentous fortune generally eats up an enormous amount of time and energy. Hence, the self-made ultra-wealthy triage with wealth creation habitually takes priority. For example, with the demands on their time due to their business dealings, they tend to make many family activities a lower priority.

Ultra-wealthy inheritors are often wrapped up within their families (see *Chapter 3: With Great Wealth Comes Great Responsibility*). On one hand, this can make some of their familial relationships very meaningful to them. On the other hand, some of their familial relationships can be extremely difficult and trying. Either way, it's normative for their familial relationships to be complicated. While this can be true of any family, the monies involved can easily add new and sometimes Byzantine sets of twists, ailments, and tribulations to the relationships.

Desirous level of control. To amass their large personal fortunes, the self-made ultra-wealthy are more likely than not to be classic, if not extreme, Type A personalities. Their conviction in what they believe in and want to attain, and their confidence in their decisions and actions, are always factors in their outstanding success. Control over their lives, their environment, and to some extent the people around them is frequently a defining characteristic.

Ultra-wealthy inheritors may or may not be as desirous for the control and are usually less so. Where they feel urgency and see themselves on a mission does the need for control become imperative. This is most evident where they're managing family enterprises, their own business ventures, and where they're focused on attaining meaningful philanthropic results.

Sourcing expertise. All the ultra-wealthy tend to turn to the professional advisors they're currently working with to introduce them to other professionals as appropriate. For the exceptionally affluent this is a very sound risk mitigation strategy. The experts they currently employ should have knowledge of and access to authorities in different fields. Moreover, relying on their judgment in these matters is logical.

Ultra-wealthy inheritors also readily turn to professionals they're currently engaging when they need to source other types of expertise (see *Chapter 9: Selecting Professional Advisors*). However, unlike the self-made ultra-wealthy, they're also somewhat inclined to turn to their peers for such introductions. The underlying rationale is that their peers, having similar experiences and having to deal with similar issues also, will know professional advisors who are likely to be helpful in these comparable situations. Additionally, they trust their peers to be forthright and candid with them.

Most probable cause of downfall. Sometimes it's as if the world is conspiring against the ultra-wealthy. For unforeseen and unforeseeable factors, great wealth can dissipate and vanish. At other times, the fiscal disasters are quite apparent, as the ultra-wealthy hit the gas, speeding up to go over the cliff.

When human error is the steadfast cause, we often see two different large-scale reasons for the disintegration of a great personal fortune. In the case of the self-made ultra-wealthy, hubris more commonly plays a starring role. By failing to understand their own weaknesses or deluding themselves that their judgment is divine (or close to divine), the self-made ultra-wealthy can make awfully poor decisions. When these decisions are combined, they act as multipliers promoting the plunge into financial oblivion.

Ultra-wealthy inheritors can also make poor decisions, but they're more commonly of a different variety. Their errors in judgment are mostly a product of a dearth of expertise and experience. In effect, they're in difficult situations with complex implications, and they're not seeking out good counsel. At times this is a function of being caught unaware by circumstances beyond their control. At other times, it's because they became distracted and failed to be appropriately attentive.

EXHIBIT 1.10 Comparing the Self-Made Ultra-Wealthy and Ultra-Wealthy Inheritors

CRITERIA	SELF-MADE	INHERITORS
Wealth creation	Core	Often of lesser importance
Family	Regularly a lower priority	Often important and complicated
Desirous level of control	Very high to extreme	Varies extensively but usually lower
Sourcing expertise	Primarily other professionals	Other professionals but peers as well
Most probable cause of downfall	Hubris	A lack of knowledge and attention

While these assessments no doubt miss many nuances and don't even accurately explain all those ultra-wealthy who are self-made or inheriting, they do help us roughly differentiate between the two segments of astounding wealth. Going forward, we're addressing ultra-wealthy inheritors. But even here, we're concentrating on those who have many similar qualities such as a strong commitment to philanthropy and a keen interest in deal making as well as possessing an honest self-reflective nature.

CONCLUSION

Relatively speaking, ultra-wealthy inheritors constitute a trans-global community. They're a quickly growing segment of the super-rich, who in taking the reins of vast family fortunes, being well educated and well connected as well as highly motivated, can potentially productively transform key aspects of our world. It's also a segment who is surrounded in anecdotes and sensational stories much of which many times proves to be outliers and some are no doubt fabrications.

Our focus in this treatise is to garner and share some decisive insights into this unique segment of the extremely affluent. To this end, we're looking at ultra-wealthy inheritors through a prism, segmenting them into individuals and those who are working at their families' single-family offices.

As we repeated a number of times, there are some substantial weaknesses to the research (see *Appendix: Limitations When Researching Wealth*) making it hard to generalize. To garner a better understanding of this elite cohort, we incorporate insights from our experience working and consulting with the ultra-wealthy. At the same time, we included insights from leading authorities in their respective fields (see *Part III: Expert Perspectives*). Still, our findings and perceptions are plagued by restraints. Nevertheless, every step forward is a step closer to having a viable understanding of this segment of extreme wealth, which has serious implications for them, the professional advisors they turn to for guidance, and for society.

INHERITING MORE THAN MONEY

MONEY ISN'T THE ONLY THING passed down to these ultra-wealthy inheritors. They like everyone else learn a lot from their elders. Sometimes the education is intended, and at other times, it's part of the fabric of their lives.

If we define the term "inheriting" as something received from predecessors, we find that ultra-wealthy inheritors get much more than money or valuables from their families. This is not just characteristic of this cohort as these qualities and attributes are regularly passed down in all families. This commonality among all families is a point we come back to a number of times. What's useful to recognize is where the similarities begin and end between the ultra-wealthy and those who have less financial resources.

INHERITING INTANGIBLES

About 90% of ultra-wealthy inheritors point to their families and the environments they grew up in as being the source of their core values (Exhibit 2.1). This is proportionately more the case with SFO ultra-wealthy inheritors. Meanwhile, few of the remainder evolved their core values to where they are today from their experiences once they were "out on their own."

Core values provide the foundation that governs a person's personal and professional relationships. They clarify who people are and act as decision-making guides. There are many potential core values, and two that stand out in this cohort are the motivation to excel and a responsibility to society.

EXHIBIT 2.1 Inherited Certain Core Values

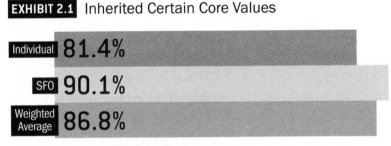

Individual **81.4%**

SFO **90.1%**

Weighted Average **86.8%**

N = 114 ultra-wealthy inheritors

About 80% of the ultra-wealthy inheritors reported inheriting a motivation to excel (Exhibit 2.2). This perspective is nearly unanimous among the SFO ultra-wealthy inheritors. In looking at these findings, it's crucial to keep in mind that the drive to accomplish, for instance, while central to the ultra-wealthy inheritors we researched, is not necessarily evident among all ultra-wealthy inheritors. Moreover, what they focus their efforts on can vary extensively.

At the same time, almost 70% report a strong sense of societal responsibility. With respect to this core value, individual ultra-wealthy inheritors are proportionately more represented.

There are a plethora of examples of very rich inheritors opting for a sybaritic and highly decadent lifestyle. We've habitually found that these individuals don't have the time or interest to take surveys usually making them absent from our research efforts.

28

EXHIBIT 2.2 Select Core Values Inherited

DRIVERS	INDIVIDUAL	SFO	WEIGHTED AVERAGE
Motivation to excel	55.8%	94.4%	79.8%
Societal responsibility	76.7%	62.0%	67.5%

N = 114 ultra-wealthy inheritors

The actualization of these values can take many forms. For example, the motivation to excel can impact everything they do or be highly selective. Similarly, while many ultra-wealthy inheritors feel they learned social responsibility from their elders, this doesn't necessarily translate into philanthropy. Their view of societal responsibility, for example, may very well be building businesses that are socially beneficial or that do very well by their employees.

What's evident is that ultra-wealthy inheritors—even those who have dramatic conflicts with their families—identify their forebearers as the source of many (not necessarily all) of their values. We're familiar with more than a few situations where the inherited core values are a function of repulsion to their parents' actions. For instance, one ultra-wealthy inheritor noting the limited amount of time and interest showed to him by his parents has identified a commitment to "family" as central to his belief system.

We've also determined that while these core values are inherited, again how ultra-wealthy inheritors actualize them may be very different than how their parents actualized them. The trend is very much to put their very personal imprint on business or charity.

What's very telling is the preponderance of ultra-wealthy inheritors expressed they're aligned with their families. This can prove advantageous or detrimental depending on the family in question. It can mean living up to the expectation of family members (see *Chapter 3: With Great Wealth Comes Great Responsibility*). It can potentially mean there's a perceived need to correct previous wrongs. Whatever the case, it's clear that for about three-quarters of them, this inheritance comes with it an array of pressures and stresses (Exhibit 2.3). Moreover, a greater percentage of the SFO ultra-wealthy inheritors feel stressed, which is probably a function of their involvement in their single-family offices.

EXHIBIT 2.3 Stress Associated With Being a Family Member

Individual **67.4%**

SFO **81.7%**

Weighted Average **76.3%**

N = 114 ultra-wealthy inheritors

Ultra-wealthy inheritors are clearly entwined within their families. If nothing else, they're often inculcated with their family's values. How these values translate into action can vary radically. While an underlying motivation may be the same across generations, such as the "need" to excel, how the different generations represent that motivation can be in diametric opposition.

CONCLUSION

Ultra-wealthy inheritors inherit more than wealth from their forebearers. Many clearly inherit core values. While they recognize they're inheriting basic beliefs and perspectives, this doesn't mean they'll be following in the steps of previous generations. For example, in the case of a wealth creator, the motivation to excel results in the formation of a substantial personal fortune. For an ultra-wealthy inheritor, that same motivation to excel can result in the creation of life-changing philanthropic endeavors.

While ultra-wealthy inheritors identify their predecessors as important influences, this doesn't mean they don't develop their own standpoints and there aren't other influencers. With this cohort we regularly find strong peer-to-peer influence that's rarely evident among significant wealth creators. This is evidenced in the way they sometimes source professional advisors (see *Chapter 9: Selecting Professional Advisors*).

3

WITH GREAT WEALTH COMES GREAT RESPONSIBILITY

THE ULTRA-WEALTHY INHERITORS in this study are lacking a "sense of entitlement." They do not perceive their financial stature to give them the right to stand above others. On the contrary, these ultra-wealthy inheritors are keenly aware of the role fate has played in their pecuniary standing. They tend to see their vast wealth as a gift. Even where they're involved in the expansion of the family fortune, they regularly understand they've been given a golden opportunity and that credit for their achievements is due, in part, to their predecessors.

These ultra-wealthy inheritors are much attuned to their family histories as well as the world around them. Many of them clearly identify an array of pressing societal, environmental, and related needs with the strong intent on bettering society. Because of their sensitivity to the world around them, they're looking to share their wealth with others—on constructive terms (see *Chapter 5: Philanthropy*).

The way this sample was constructed and, in part, the reason many agreed to participate in the research was because they're strongly philanthropically inclined. While this certainly creates boundaries to the results (see *Appendix: Limitations Researching Wealth*), many of the insights and conclusions are, nevertheless, quite telling leading to actionable strategies and educational opportunities.

DOING SOMETHING SIGNIFICANT

We find that nearly nine out of ten of the ultra-wealthy desire to do something significant in the world with no difference of note between the two segments (Exhibit 3.1). It's important to recognize that there's tremendous potential variation possible when addressing doing something significant. This can take many forms and is tightly related to the responsibilities they've identified for themselves.

EXHIBIT 3.1 Desire to Do Something Significant in the World

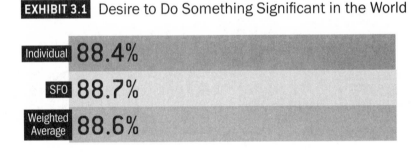

Individual **88.4%**

SFO **88.7%**

Weighted Average **88.6%**

N = 114 ultra-wealthy inheritors

When it comes to the topic of responsibilities, we can divide them into three major categories—family, wealth, and philanthropy. Each of these sets of responsibilities draws the attention and energies of ultra-wealthy inheritors.

FAMILY

A major responsibility for about half the ultra-wealthy inheritors is dealing effectively with family obligations (Exhibit 3.2). There's a major difference between individual ultra-wealthy inheritors and SFO ultra-wealthy inheritors in this regard.

These family obligations can be anything from being appropriately respectful at family functions to preparing to take over their single-family offices. What's clear is that these individuals feeling this way are psychologically embedded within their families and see the need to perpetuate the family agenda or to expand the family's role beyond where it stands today. The way this is accomplished can freely result in meaningful changes to the family's character.

The nature of these family obligations is idiosyncratic to the particular family. Nevertheless, they are determinants in the goals and objectives of the ultra-wealthy inheritors. As with all families the ability to "live up to" the expectations of parents, for example, can prove difficult. Many of these family obligations are self-determined such as looking out for siblings who feel they don't need being looked after and can deal with life on their own terms. Without question, not everything likely runs smoothly in their familial lives, and the monies involved can often add to the complications.

EXHIBIT 3.2 Need to Address Family Obligations

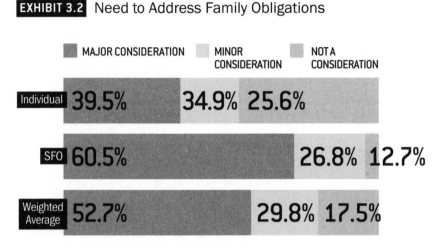

N = 114 ultra-wealthy inheritors

While there is a superfluity of advantages to being born into a world of great wealth, there are some drawbacks as well. But then again, conceptually these drawbacks are no different than those faced by families where riches are not a defining element. Unsurprisingly, two-fifths of those surveyed frequently have disagreements with their family concerning how they should live their lives (Exhibit 3.3). Relatively speaking, more of the individual ultra-wealthy inheritors are more likely to have such conflicts than SFO ultra-wealthy inheritors. For about half those surveyed, such conflicts happen frequently. About 8% rarely have such conflicts.

This entails the plethora of decisions such as their role in the family business, the people they associate with including potential spouses, and even the charitable causes they do or should support. For example, being on opposite sides of the political spectrum between generations is not unknown and is always a cause of deep frustration on both sides.

EXHIBIT 3.3 Conflicting Expectations With Important Family

N = 114 ultra-wealthy inheritors

In various ways, many of these ultra-wealthy inheritors are closely bonded with their families. The existence of interlocking business interests, trusts, and other structures controlling family assets can readily create financial and lifestyle co-dependency relationships that range in their beneficial nature. Issues within families are pervasive irrespective of wealth. However, great wealth can very well magnify and accentuate conflicts and skew expectations to an even greater extent than otherwise.

What can be quite deleterious to ultra-wealthy inheritors is a failure to accurately understand these matters. Instead, by appreciating the dynamics, family expectations and obligations, ultra-wealthy inheritors can triage so that the considerations and concerns that really matter can be attended to as well as effectively psychologically dealt with.

WEALTH

While often intersecting with family obligations, about 90% of the ultra-wealthy inheritors are focused on their own professional goals (Exhibit 3.4). This is somewhat more prevalent among the SFO ultra-wealthy inheritors and is likely to be a function of their involvement in their single-family offices.

This desire can also run the gamut from successfully managing family and/or non-family corporate interests to launching and managing their own ventures to striking off in a different professional direction entirely. Whichever the course, this cohort is generally motivated to work hard and commit themselves to achieving their professional agendas.

EXHIBIT 3.4 Desire to Achieve Own Professional Goals

Individual **79.1%**

SFO **93.0%**

Weighted Average **87.9%**

N = 114 ultra-wealthy inheritors

Tied to their focus on professional achievements, about 85% of ultra-wealthy inheritors are strongly motivated to become significantly personally wealthier, and this finding is more common among the SFO ultra-wealthy inheritors (Exhibit 3.5). With money regularly being the scorecard of professional accomplishments, the desire for more might have little to do with "how much is enough" or accumulating to spend. Instead, it's regularly about demonstrating business acumen and financial proficiencies. It's usually a sign of their competencies.

EXHIBIT 3.5 Desire to Become Significantly Personally Wealthier

Individual **65.1%**

SFO **95.8%**

Weighted Average **84.2%**

N = 114 ultra-wealthy inheritors

PHILANTHROPY

For ultra-wealthy inheritors there are also issues concerning their obligations to the world at large. As such, many of them express a desire to do something significant because they're confident they can "make a difference" (see above). Tied to this perspective is the general consensus that wealth and philanthropy go hand in hand (Exhibit 3.6). It's positive recognition of Noblesse Oblige. Again, while this perspective is not unique to the very wealthy, their pecuniary resources can enable them to do things many others cannot. This issue is discussed further in *Chapter 5: Philanthropy*.

EXHIBIT 3.6 Believe that Those Who Are Wealthier
Must Be Philanthropic

Individual **88.4%**

SFO **79.8%**

Weighted Average **82.5%**

N = 114 ultra-wealthy inheritors

To achieve these ambitions necessitates having the drive as well as knowledge and skills. It's quite evident that many of ultra-wealthy inheritors are astoundingly motivated to tackle their responsibilities. While we readily recognize that great fortunes have bred many "trust babies," the cohort we queried does not fall into that category. To reiterate, finding these ultra-wealthy inheritors are, to a large degree, solidly philanthropic is probabilistically tied to the sampling methodology (see *Chapter 1: Ultra-Wealthy Inheritors; Appendix: Limitations Researching Wealth*).

CONCLUSION

As the title of this chapter details, wealth can foster the need to make a difference. This might be in the context of their families, business and—for these ultra-wealthy inheritors—very possibly, the world.

These responsibilities that have been handed to them, or they took on themselves, do not distinguish them from other people. The desire to help family members in need or make the world a better place is not, in any way, the restricted province of great wealth. The difference is the range of actions that are possible.

Money—especially vast amounts of money—can be highly instrumental in addressing these responsibilities when used by thoughtful, intelligent, and surprisingly clever individuals. By combining the power of large fortunes and marvelous connections with the powerful, influential, and considerate, ultra-wealthy inheritors have the lever and the location to potentially move the world.

4

ENHANCING
EXPERTISE

WHILE MANY ULTRA-WEALTHY INHERITORS HAVE

taken charge, or anticipate doing so, of personal and family monies and obligations, a solid percentage of them recognize that they're not completely prepared to deal with some of their obligations and opportunities. It's not about their limitations as much as it's about areas where greater proficiency translates into substantially greater advantages (see *Chapter 11: The Education of Global Stewards*).

Through the survey, we identified a number of areas where the ultra-wealthy inheritors felt a greater refinement or enhancement of their knowledge and abilities would prove valuable. These areas can be divided into process and technical expertise.

When it comes to process expertise, ultra-wealthy inheritors tend to be very interested in being able to negotiate with considerable proficiency. Their objective is to be able to bargain more efficaciously. Concurrently, being able to make the best use of their generally very expansive and powerful networks is another area where many are looking to become more adept.

With respect to technical expertise, we're dealing with the ability to act on their own as well as accurately and effectively understand and follow what the professional advisors they hire are doing for them and their families. Whether these professional advisors are money managers or investment bankers or tax lawyers or personal security specialists, the key is being able to understand what they're actually doing and to match the current actions and intended outcomes with definable results.

As we'll see, most ultra-wealthy inheritors tend to want to have a meaningful grasp concerning the actions of these professional advisors, while some are or aim to take on select roles themselves.

Let's begin with process expertise.

PROCESS EXPERTISE

When it comes to process expertise, we're looking at the mind-set and behaviors that enable ultra-wealthy inheritors to be more effective in various business and personal environments. The areas where we've conducted a considerable amount of research and where we extensively consult with the ultra-wealthy as well as those fast-tracking to extreme wealth is how to most effectively negotiate and network.

Bargaining brilliance. While capable, about 60% of the ultra-wealthy inheritors are very interested in becoming more able negotiators. (Exhibit 4.1). Being more facile in this regard produces a multitude of benefits.

Skilled negotiating can be quite important in all aspects of business from buying and selling companies or other assets (see *Chapter 7: Doing Deals*) to building a world-class collection (see *Chapter 12: Ultra-Wealthy Connoisseurs*) to achieving significant charitable objectives (see *Chapter 5: Philanthropy*). It's also an instrumental ability to be able to derive the greatest benefits from working with talented experts (see *Chapter 9: Selecting Professional Advisors*).

Another benefit of being more skillful negotiators concerns their families. Accomplished bargaining enhances the opportunities to move beyond the perceptions of certain family members and work on matters of substance especially in business scenarios. As with numerous aspects of the business lives of ultra-wealthy inheritors, while many are quite competent, a fairly large percentage is nevertheless looking to become ever more accomplished.

EXHIBIT 4.1 Become Better Negotiators

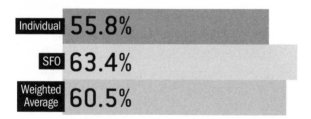

Individual 55.8%

SFO 63.4%

Weighted Average 60.5%

N = 114 ultra-wealthy inheritors

What's very telling is that a strong interest in improving their negotiating abilities is endemic among a large percentage of the wealthy and successful. While many of these individuals are quite proficient, there's still the desire to ratchet their expertise ever higher. This widespread wish has led us to synthesize the mind-set and best practices of extraordinarily successful negotiators whose bargaining proficiencies have significantly contributed to their financial achievements.

Based on extensive quantitative and qualitative work with the self-made wealthy whose negotiating ability was (and is) instrumental in creating sizable personal fortunes, we identified a methodology employed across the board by this cohort that we refer to as *bargaining brilliance*. The fact that we can dissect the thinking and actions of the accomplished wealthy, and—extremely importantly—educate others on how to follow in their footsteps means that this highly effective approach to negotiating is not in any way innate (see *Chapter 13: Bargaining Brilliance*). On the contrary, it's highly learnable and is often embedded in the various curriculums we develop.

Street-smart networking. Aside from becoming more proficient negotiators, three-quarters of ultra-wealthy inheritors are highly interested in becoming more adept at leveraging their unusually robust and often exceptionally extensive network of personal and professional relationships (Exhibit 4.2). This is proportionately more the case among SFO ultra-wealthy inheritors.

Through family, school, philanthropic, business, and personal contacts, ultra-wealthy inheritors are generally well "wired." Besides knowing people considering their financial positions, it many times can be easy to obtain an effective introduction to someone they don't know but want to meet.

EXHIBIT 4.2   Become Better at Leveraging Their Networks

Individual **60.5%**

SFO **84.5%**

Weighted Average **75.4%**

N = 114 ultra-wealthy inheritors

One way to assess the nature of their networks is to look at their participation on boards of directors and advisory boards (Exhibit 4.3). About half of them are on company boards, which are more so for the SFO ultra-wealthy inheritors. Similarly, about half of ultra-wealthy inheritors are on some sort of charity board, which is more likely among individual ultra-wealthy inheritors. A more modest fifth of them have these positions in membership organizations.

Aside from the influence these board positions generate, the ability to connect with other board members, for example, ofttimes leads to significant business opportunities. Because of being on boards of directors or advisory boards, many of the ultra-wealthy inheritors have the opportunity to translate these situations into commercial and charitable possibilities.

EXHIBIT 4.3   Board (Director or Advisory) Memberships

DRIVERS	INDIVIDUAL	SFO	WEIGHTED AVERAGE
Companies	**41.9%**	**62.0%**	**54.4%**
Eleemosynary organizations	**58.1%**	**46.5%**	**50.9%**
Membership organizations	**20.9%**	**21.1%**	**21.1%**

N = 114 ultra-wealthy inheritors

Another way for ultra-wealthy inheritors to network with like-minded and equally wealthy individuals is at conclaves. These gatherings range broadly from events such as attending the annual meeting of The World Economic Forum to the multitude of smaller educational and business events produced by professional advisors.

Nine out of ten of the ultra-wealthy inheritors participated in conclaves—of one kind or another—within the last five years (Exhibit 4.4). Aside from being a common way for the very wealthy to associate, we suspect the way we built this sample favors those who do indeed participate in conclaves (see *Appendix: Limitations When Researching Wealth*).

Conclaves of every variety certainly provide opportunities for ultra-wealthy inheritors to expand their networks and deepen their relationships. In fact, when we produce educational programs for the ultra-wealthy including inheritors, we structure them to foster multi-level, results-driven sharing with their peers while delivering actionable solutions.

EXHIBIT 4.4   Participated in Conclaves and Similar "Events"— Last Five Years

Individual	**76.7%**
SFO	**97.2%**
Weighted Average	**89.5%**

N = 114 ultra-wealthy inheritors

It's undeniable that the majority of ultra-wealthy inheritors are extremely well connected. While some of them are amazingly skilled at leveraging these relationships, there are those who aren't as capable. Whether for business or charitable purposes, a meaningful percentage of them are interested in being more proficient at benefiting from their close and extended relationships. What these ultra-wealthy inheritors are looking for are ways to make better use of their networks and networking potential.

All in all, while ultra-wealthy inheritors are exceptionally well connected, some of them sometimes find their ability to develop ways to monetize their extensive relationships, for example, to be more limited than they would like. We've found that the ultra-wealthy overall can derive tremendous advantages by systematically structuring their networks including creating Advocates (see *Chapter 14: Street-Smart Networking*).

TECHNICAL EXPERTISE

When it comes to technical expertise, a different kind of learning is attractive for some of the ultra-wealthy inheritors. In contrast, to process expertise where the ultra-wealthy inheritors are looking to enhance their mastery in certain interpersonal arenas, they're more interested in understanding the basics and the "big picture" as it relates to the financial, legal and related activities they're involved with. While this varies with respect to different sets of expertise, in the aggregate their focus is predominately on the fundamentals delegating the "doing" to the appropriate experts (Exhibit 4.5).

Specifically, about half the ultra-wealthy inheritors want a basic understanding of the technical issues. The SFO ultra-wealthy inheritors tend to want have a far greater understanding of the technical issues than the individual ultra-wealthy inheritors.

EXHIBIT 4.5 Interest in Understanding the Technical Issues

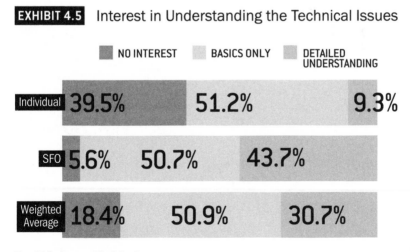

NO INTEREST   BASICS ONLY   DETAILED UNDERSTANDING

	NO INTEREST	BASICS ONLY	DETAILED UNDERSTANDING
Individual	39.5%	51.2%	9.3%
SFO	5.6%	50.7%	43.7%
Weighted Average	18.4%	50.9%	30.7%

N = 114 ultra-wealthy inheritors

The rationale for having baseline knowledge of some of these technical areas is to mitigate the chances of being taken advantage of or exploited. Many of them or their families were taken advantage of within the last half dozen years (see *Chapter 9: Selecting Professional Advisors*). Their goal is not to necessarily personally replace the services of these professional advisors. While many are not looking to be the tax expert or act as a close protection specialist, they still want to have a basic understanding of these professional services.

CONCLUSION

What is evident is that some ultra-wealthy inheritors desire to further expand and refine their knowledge and skills. The ability to negotiate at a truly high-caliber level is a critical capability and one where many feel they can improve. The ability to bargain effectively impacts all aspects of their professional and personal lives and can make a meaningful difference in their success.

The ability to exponentially leverage their personal, family, and business networks is recognized by many ultra-wealthy inheritors as an opportunity from which they're not fully benefitting. While they know lots of people—many of them powerful and highly influential—the capability to convert these relationships into greater results is occasionally out of their grasp. We know that when ultra-wealthy inheritors can artfully manage their myriad and extensive relationships, they're able to achieve especially powerful outcomes (see *Chapter 14: Street-Smart Networking*).

With respect to technical matters, most ultra-wealthy inheritors are happy to take a watch and use it to tell the time, having limited interest in the mechanism of the watch. Although a percentage of ultra-wealthy inheritors especially the SFO ultra-wealthy inheritors, by inclination, drive, or business necessity are concerned about the mechanics of the technical services they use.

PART II
Taking the Reins

CHAPTER
5

PHILANTHROPY

philanthropy is a defining characteristic. It's not just about giving and "doing good," it's increasingly about making a significant positive impact on the world or some component of it (see *Chapter 3: With Great Wealth Comes Great Responsibility*).

A number of factors contribute to the philanthropic motivations of ultra-wealthy inheritors. Included here are:

- The belief that those who can be philanthropic should.

- An inherited core value.

- Sociological factors as evidenced by their interest in the way other members of their cohort are approaching philanthropy.

Because of the way the sample was constructed (see *Chapter 1: Ultra-Wealthy Inheritors; Appendix: Limitations When Researching Wealth*), for many of these ultra-wealthy inheritors, their interest in philanthropy was a forgone conclusion. However, there's a gap between wanting to be constructively philanthropic and being as constructively philanthropic as they would like.

RECOGNIZING THE NEED TO DO BETTER

While making concerted efforts to be philanthropic, 65% of ultra-wealthy inheritors believe they can do a better job (Exhibit 5.1). They recognize opportunities to be more strategic and more effective. This perspective is more pervasive among individual ultra-wealthy inheritors.

EXHIBIT 5.1   Can Do a Better Job Being Philanthropic

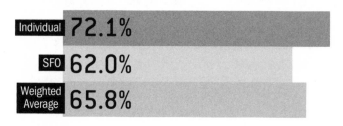

Individual **72.1%**

SFO **62.0%**

Weighted Average **65.8%**

N = 114 ultra-wealthy inheritors

Part of the problem may be that only about a quarter of the ultra-wealthy inheritors have clearly defined philanthropic goals (Exhibit 5.2). Those with such goals know just what they want to accomplish and are very attuned to the ways they can meet these expectations. Very often this incorporates the structures they employ such as foundations and trusts to achieve their charitable agendas.

More telling is that about half the ultra-wealthy inheritors have only "directional philanthropic goals." It's more than knowing they want to do something and sometimes what this might entail, writ large, but it's less than being precisely aware of what specifically they want to accomplish and how. Many times this lack of specificity is due to a desire not to close off options and, as of yet, in contrast to drilling down into the details.

Lastly, about one-fifth of them are somewhat in the dark. They haven't identified a charitable cause(s) they're truly excited about supporting.

EXHIBIT 5.2 Philanthropic Goals

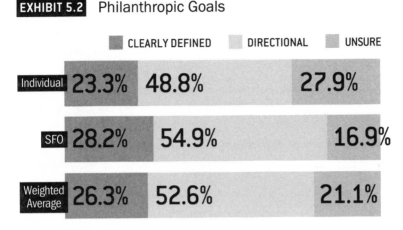

N = 114 ultra-wealthy inheritors

CONNECTING WITH OTHER PHILANTHROPISTS

While we've found some extreme commitments to charitable causes among ultra-wealthy inheritors because of the monies at their command, they're often open to other possibilities. This extends beyond various charitable causes to the mechanics of being philanthropic. Thus, nearly three-quarters of them are interested in how other wealthy families and individuals are approaching philanthropy (Exhibit 5.3).

This overall strong interest in how other ultra-wealthy families are approaching philanthropy is characteristic of ultra-wealthy inheritors in general. By and large, they're highly motivated to understand what their peers are doing across a spectrum of activities and endeavors. By sharing with their peers, ultra-wealthy inheritors are able to expeditiously move up the learning curve.

EXHIBIT 5.3 Interested in Learning How Other Ultra-Wealthy Families are Approaching Philanthropy

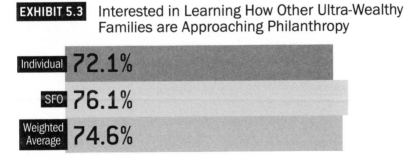

N = 114 ultra-wealthy inheritors

In this scenario as well as in many others, ultra-wealthy inheritors are more inclined than extreme wealth creators in turning to their peers so as to learn from their experiences. For example, this distinction is very evident in the greater probability of ultra-wealthy inheritors turning to their peers in sourcing professional advisors, something extreme wealth creators are highly unlikely to do (see *Chapter 1: Ultra-Wealthy Inheritors*).

Paralleling this perspective, about seven out of ten ultra-wealthy inheritors are highly interested in being introduced to likeminded individuals (Exhibit 5.4). The objective is often one or more of the following:

- To learn of interesting opportunities and possibilities.

- To access resources and expertise.

- To learn about best practices in various functional areas.

EXHIBIT 5.4   Highly Interested in Being Introduced to Likeminded Individuals

Individual **65.1%**

SFO **71.8%**

Weighted Average **69.3%**

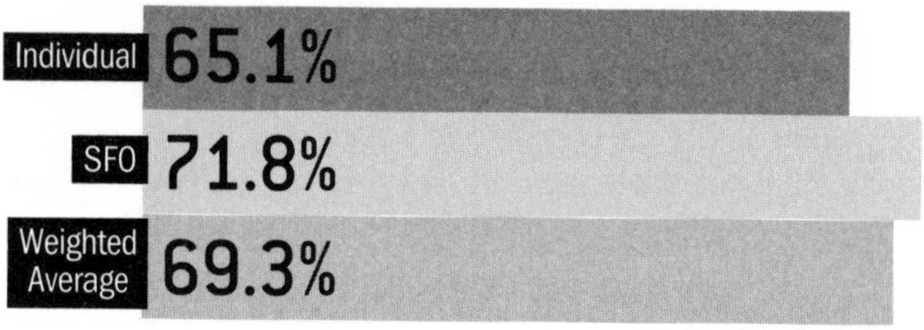

N = 114 ultra-wealthy inheritors

In sum, we find that many ultra-wealthy inheritors are actively seeking out ways to enable them to use their fortunes to make meaningful differences. A principal way they're looking to make a difference is to understand potential opportunities and methods by learning how their peers are approaching philanthropy.

What's also evident is that ultra-wealthy inheritors are very intent on making the philanthropic decisions.

TAKING THE REINS

Many ultra-wealthy inheritors are motivated to be philanthropic. Moreover, they're motivated to take a leadership role when it comes to their charitable endeavors (Exhibit 5.5). About three-quarters of them expect to be extensively involved in deciding which charitable causes to support.

EXHIBIT 5.5 Will Become Significantly More Involved in Deciding
Which Charities to Support

Individual **88.4%**

SFO **63.4%**

Weighted Average **72.8%**

N = 114 ultra-wealthy inheritors

For ultra-wealthy inheritors, it's not enough to back worthwhile causes. By and large, their intent is to get results (Exhibit 5.6). About half of them expect to play a role in making their philanthropic projects more effective. Also, nearly seven out of ten are highly concerned about evaluating the impact and results of their giving. Hence, they're able to fine-tune their philanthropic activities. This is more characteristic of SFO ultra-wealthy inheritors.

EXHIBIT 5.6 Will Become Significantly More Involved
in Getting Results

INVOLVEMENT	INDIVIDUAL	SFO	WEIGHTED AVERAGE
Making philanthropic endeavors work more effectively	53.5%	46.5%	49.1%
Evaluating the impact and result of giving	62.8%	70.4%	67.5%

N = 114 ultra-wealthy inheritors

For many ultra-wealthy inheritors, it's not only about charitable causes and ensuring their monies are being used wisely and effectively. It's also about making sure their monies are working as hard as possible.

MAKING CHARITABLE MONIES WORK HARDER

There are numerous ways to make donated monies "do more." This is not about getting better results from giving. Instead, it's about getting better results from the management of funds they donate. What we find is that about 30% of the ultra-wealthy are presently taking steps to maximize the monies they donate (Exhibit 5.7). To date, SFO ultra-wealthy inheritors are more inclined to do so.

EXHIBIT 5.7 Financially Maximize the Monies Donated

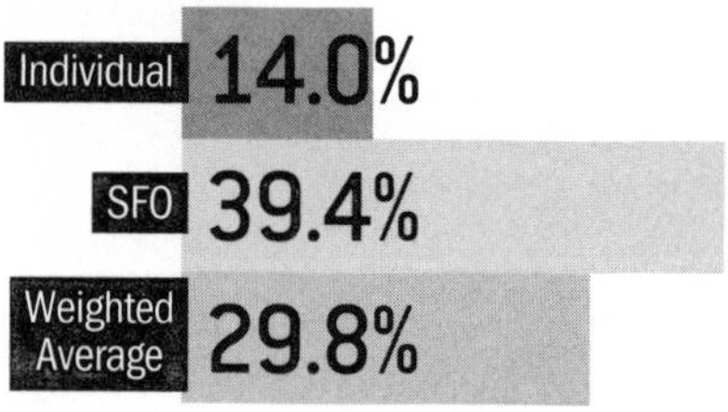

Individual **14.0**%

SFO **39.4%**

Weighted Average **29.8%**

N = 114 ultra-wealthy inheritors

There are likely a variety of reasons for this such as an inability to use certain financial strategies because of the legal structures being employed. However, the most pervasive reason for not maximizing the monies donated is a lack of knowledge. It's a dearth of expertise in this specialized field that's usually the major hurdle to the ultra-wealthy being able to be more financially astute with their charitable funds. Nearly 65% of ultra-wealthy inheritors are strongly interested in learning how to leverage philanthropic monies (Exhibit 5.8). There's greater interest in this among SFO ultra-wealthy inheritors.

EXHIBIT 5.8 Strongly Interested in Learning How to Leverage Philanthropic Monies

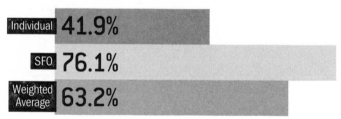

Individual **41.9%**

SFO **76.1%**

Weighted Average **63.2%**

N = 114 ultra-wealthy inheritors

There are a number of ways to leverage philanthropic monies. On the personal side, various trusts—depending on the tax code—can transform assets to greater charitable dollars than direct donations. For respect to private foundations, some examples of leveraging philanthropic dollars include:

- Issuing debt.

- Incorporating charitable life insurance on a corporate basis.

- Hedging portfolios.

What's important is for ultra-wealthy inheritors to be able to make informed decisions. This necessitates they're properly informed and understand the consequences of their options.

CONCLUSION

Many of the ultra-wealthy are solidly philanthropic. The impediments come in actualizing their agendas complicated by the fact for a percentage of them, there is a lack of clarity concerning their agendas. We find that a substantial number of ultra-wealthy inheritors are looking to make a significant societal difference and some are seeking guidance. Their ability to connect with their peers as well as other likeminded individuals is important to many of them.

What's quite evident is that many are looking to chart their own philanthropic course. This will involve the selection of charitable causes as well as the way to support them. Included here is the ability to maximize their financial commitments.

WEALTH
MANAGEMENT

ACCESSING AND IMPLEMENTING the full range of interrelated
financial services and expertise is known as *wealth management*. When it comes to the
ultra-wealthy, a comprehensive wealth management platform generally incorporates:

- Financial and legal analyses
- Investment management
- Advanced planning
- Business and investment transactions

- Credit and basic banking services
- Insurances
- Currency management
- Private investment banking

We queried ultra-wealthy inheritors about investment management, advance
planning, and deal making. In our experience, these areas of wealth management
tend to be important, fairly pervasive, and highly variable with respect to the
ultra-wealthy. Because of the extensive expertise required to meet the needs and
wants of ultra-wealthy inheritors, a well-orchestrated team of experts is required to
deliver these solutions. Very often, a particular professional advisor or small team of
professional advisors, who understands and works closely with ultra-wealthy
inheritors, coordinates these various technical specialists.

SIX CORE ELEMENTS

Underpinning top-of-the-line wealth management are six principles. The extent to which ultra-wealthy inheritors capitalize on these elements is often a function of the way their assets have been handed down to them, their knowledge, and perspectives as well as their family obligations (see *Chapter 3: With Great Wealth Comes Great Responsibility*). The following are the six principles:

• **Maximum flexibility** is needed in order to be able to deal with an ever-quickening interrelated political, economic, and social environment. Undeniably, from "lives in trust" to rock hard illiquid long-term investments, there are limits to flexibility. However, astute wealth management for the ultra-wealthy needs to build in a reasonable amount of tractability based on the realization of unknown circumstances.

• **Internal transparency** is called for in order to address matters of interpersonal trust. Ultra-wealthy inheritors are wise not to blindly rely on others as their lifestyles, fortunes, and critically, their dreams and agendas can be easily compromised (see *Chapter 9: Selecting Professional Advisors*).

• **Cohesiveness** where the various investments and legal actions all work together as best as possible. Optimal wealth management results are often accomplished when there's an overarching understanding of what's going on and, moreover, there's integration.

• **Risk sensitivity** describes the degree to which investments and legal strategies are appropriate based on the specific risk tolerances of the ultra-wealthy inheritors. It's very much a question of carefully evaluating the downside of various wealth management actions with particular attention to their impact on selected other family members and circumstances.

• **Cost effectiveness** refers to balancing the benefits of investments and legal actions with their anticipated outcomes. The financial, psychological, familial, and social costs should always be taken into account. In one respect, it's a matter of choosing the course of action that gets the desired results and costs the least to implement and live with.

• **Legitimacy** means that everything done is squarely within the parameters of the law. In principle, this is a non-issue. In practice, meanwhile, it can prove very complicated and sometimes problematic. This is due to the various legal jurisdictions in which ultra-wealthy inheritors live and operate (see *Chapter 1: Ultra-Wealthy Inheritors*). Nevertheless, it's a given that there's constantly a fastidious attention to abiding by all the laws and regulations.

Let's now consider investment management and advanced planning. Because of the considerable interest ultra-wealthy inheritors have in deal making, we'll look at that topic in the following chapter.

INVESTMENT MANAGEMENT

The ultra-wealthy—many times—have a portion of their wealth in a liquid investment portfolio (see *Chapter 1: Ultra-Wealth Inheritors*). While the matter of liquidity varies considering gates in alternative investment funds, for instance, what we have are assets that can be more readily converted to cash.

With respect to investment management, today very few of the individual ultra-wealthy inheritors are personally involved in managing the investment portfolio or selecting money managers (Exhibit 6.1). It's a very different situation when it comes to SFO ultra-wealthy inheritors by the very nature of their positions and roles.

EXHIBIT 6.1 Very Involved Today

INVOLVEMENT	INDIVIDUAL	SFO	WEIGHTED AVERAGE
In managing your own or family's investment portfolio	7.0%	56.3%	37.7%
Selecting professional advisors to manage your own or family's investment portfolio	11.6%	84.5%	57.0%

N = 114 ultra-wealthy inheritors

What's clear is that a greater percentage of ultra-wealthy inheritors are inclined to take the reins (Exhibit 6.2). About 12% of the individual ultra-wealthy inheritors expect to become more directly involved in managing their own or their family's investment portfolio. At the same time, more of the SFO ultra-wealthy inheritors are going to become involved to a greater degree.

Looking forward, nearly nine out of ten of the ultra-wealthy inheritors anticipate becoming more involved in selecting the professional advisors who will be managing their own or their families' monies. This is resulting in ultra-wealthy inheritors adopting a more systematic approach to choosing money managers (see *Chapter 9: Selecting Professional Advisors*).

EXHIBIT 6.2 Will Become Significantly More Involved

INVOLVEMENT	INDIVIDUAL	SFO	WEIGHTED AVERAGE
In managing your own or family's investment portfolio	11.6%	60.6%	42.1%
Selecting professional advisors to manage your own or family's investment portfolio	72.1%	94.4%	86.0%

N = 114 ultra-wealthy inheritors

In the future, ultra-wealthy inheritors are probably going to have a greater say in their own or their family's investment portfolio. This is going to have numerous implications especially as they adopt potentially different investment philosophies. One such investment philosophy gaining traction with this cohort is impact investing.

Impact investing. An area of investment management we're seeing growing interest by the ultra-wealthy is impact investing. Impact investors are actively providing monies to businesses that are seeking to provide solutions most traditional philanthropic activities cannot adequately address. These investments take a number of forms including equity, debt and loan guarantees.

Presently, only about one-fifth of ultra-wealthy inheritors are actively engaged in impact investing at some level (Exhibit 6.3). However, we anticipate a boost in the number of this cohort looking to manage a portion of their liquid assets with an eye to the social good. Approaching 70% of the ultra-wealthy are interested in learning more about impact investing or seeing more investment opportunities in this area.

EXHIBIT 6.3 Impact Investing

INVOLVEMENT	INDIVIDUAL	SFO	WEIGHTED AVERAGE
Currently engaged	20.9%	21.1%	21.1%
Interested in learning more or seeing more opportunities	76.7%	62.0%	67.5%

N = 114 ultra-wealthy inheritors

Impact investing dovetails with their desire to make a significant difference (see *Chapter 3: With Great Wealth Comes Great Responsibility*) as well as their strong interest in philanthropy (see *Chapter 5: Philanthropy*). It's very clear that many ultra-wealthy inheritors are inclined to direct a portion of their wealth to viable investment that also addresses social issues.

ADVANCED PLANNING

Using legal strategies and approaches to alleviate tax burden, deal with regulations, and mitigate the probability and consequences of unfair lawsuits, all fall under the rubric of advanced planning. Generally speaking for the ultra-wealthy, the importance of advanced planning cannot be overstated. It's certainly a potentially obscure, enormously technical set of specialties, but their impact on the current and future state of the fortunes of the ultra-wealthy is pronounced.

Various types of legal planning are considered advanced planning including estate and wealth transfer, financial succession planning, tax-wise charitable giving, income tax planning, and asset protection planning (see *Chapter 15: Owning the Trust: How to Maintain Control and Flexibility; Chapter 16: Sophisticated Advanced Planning Using Life Insurance*). Because advanced planning is predicated on the laws and regulations in one or many jurisdictions, the solutions available to ultra-wealthy inheritors vary greatly.

We find that a third of ultra-wealthy inheritors are involved in sourcing specific advanced planning solutions (Exhibit 6.4). This breaks down to less than one in ten individual ultra-wealthy inheritors and a little more than half the SFO ultra-wealthy inheritors.

EXHIBIT 6.4 Involved in Sourcing Specific Advanced Planning Solutions

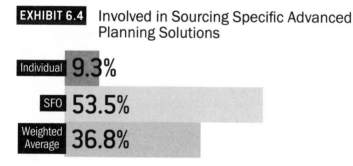

Individual **9.3%**

SFO **53.5%**

Weighted Average **36.8%**

N = 114 ultra-wealthy inheritors

On the other hand, about 95% report it's very important that they understand the outcomes of advanced planning including nearly all the SFO ultra-wealthy inheritors (Exhibit 6.5). As noted in *Chapter 3: With Great Wealth Comes Great Responsibility,* and as we'll see in *Chapter 9: Selecting Professional Advisors*, when it comes to highly technical matters, many ultra-wealthy inheritors want to comprehend the big picture and understand the pertinent details as well as oversee the experts, but many are not interested in becoming technically proficient themselves.

EXHIBIT 6.5   Understand the Outcomes of Advanced Planning

Individual **88.4%**

SFO **98.6%**

Weighted Average **94.7%**

N = 114 ultra-wealthy inheritors

Advanced planning in its various iterations is wisely integrated into all aspects of wealth management In the case of investment management, it's preferable to have greater after-tax results than a greater investment return that delivers less after taxes making private placement life insurance appealing (see *Chapter 16: Sophisticated Advanced Planning Using Life Insurance*). Similarly, the ability to sell a company and pocket appreciably more is ofttimes possible when advanced planners are brought in to structure the ownership of the assets pre-sale.

High-caliber experts are required to achieve desired results in these highly specialized areas. Unless the ultra-wealthy inheritor pursued a career in tax law, for example, he or she is not going to be the person devising the wealthy family's tax strategy.

One component of advanced planning that's garnering ever-greater interest from the ultra-wealthy is asset protection planning.

Asset protection planning. It's a discrete form of legal planning. At the same time, it's derivative of other forms of planning and related disciplines such as risk management.

The goal of asset protection planning is to provide ultra-wealthy inheritors with a viable and justifiable defense against litigants and creditors. This becomes all the more important when considering the increasing litigious nature of much of society and the too common willingness of many juries, for instance, to side against those with significant personal resources.

For asset protection solutions to be effective, timing is a major consideration. It's often essential to put asset protection strategies in place before they're needed. Thus, asset protection planning is a form of pre-litigation planning. Even though there are ways—depending on jurisdictions—to use asset protection solutions after the fact, this is often not optimal.

Being unfairly sued is not that uncommon in the environment and experiences of ultra-wealthy inheritors (Exhibit 6.6). Personally, 15% of them have been inappropriately sued. When it comes to people close to them including family, friends, and business associates, the percentage go up to 80%.

EXHIBIT 6.6 Unfairly Sued

INVOLVEMENT	INDIVIDUAL	SFO	WEIGHTED AVERAGE
Personally	18.6%	12.7%	14.9%
People close to you	72.1%	85.9%	80.7%

N = 114 ultra-wealthy inheritors

Again, depending on circumstances, such lawsuits might or might not be a concern for ultra-wealthy inheritors. Where they're a concern, high-caliber asset protection planning cannot ward off unjust and frivolous lawsuits. What they can do is provide obstacles that can make the success of the opposing side very hard to achieve. This tends to motivate them to back down in part or in total. Moreover, it creates legitimate barriers that can mitigate or eliminate possible financial obligations.

CONCLUSION

When it comes to managing their wealth and addressing relevant tax matters, ultra-wealthy inheritors are increasingly looking to play a role. With respect to investment management, the likely way most of them will become more involved is in selecting the professional advisors to manage their monies.

Ultra-wealthy inheritors are also interested in impact investing. This is, in part, a function of the way the sample was constructed (see *Appendix: Limitations When Researching Wealth*). Still, the ability to marry doing good and financial returns has a lot of appeal for this cohort.

While mitigating taxes is a major concern, ultra-wealthy inheritors are generally comfortable leaving the nuts-and-bolts of this to talented and capable legal and financial experts. However, they do want to understand the implications of the various tax strategies they might or are employing. Meantime, there's a very powerful interest in asset protection planning due to the possibility they'll be targeted because of their wealth.

7

DOING DEALS

THE BUYING AND SELLING of significant assets such as businesses or real estate or intellectual property technically falls under the umbrella of wealth management. What makes it worthy of a chapter of its own is the considerable interest ultra-wealthy inheritors have in doing deals.

Deals—in one form or another—are a principal way the ultra-wealthy become ultra-wealthy. This fact has not been lost on this cohort. Moreover, across the high-net-worth universe, deal making continues to dominate among those who are looking to seriously magnify their wealth.

THE APPEAL OF DIRECT INVESTING

It's quite common for many of the ultra-wealthy to have invested in various fund structures that subsequently invest in private companies or other assets. This scenario is not going to change dramatically in the near future. However, the exceptionally affluent are sometimes disenchanted with this approach to investing in private companies for a number of reasons including:

- The management and performance fees charged by these funds.

- The less than stellar returns garnered by some of these funds of late.

- The lack of liquidity due to lock-ups enforced by these funds.

While we're seeing a growing disgruntlement by a percentage of the ultra-wealthy investing through funds, the attraction of investing in private companies, infrastructure, real estate and other similar types of assets, however, has not abated. On the contrary, we're finding more and more very wealthy individuals looking to source and participate in a wide variety of deals.

Deal making by the ultra-wealthy appears to be a constant. For instance, they have been directly investing in companies all along, sometimes as classic angel investors and, at other times, they're working through dedicated corporate structures such as single-family offices or through their own private equity funds. Presently, a little more than one-fifth of the ultra-wealthy inheritors are involved in some kind of deal-making activities, and SFO ultra-wealthy inheritors dominate these activities (Exhibit 7.1).

EXHIBIT 7.1 Currently Doing Deals

Individual **7.0%**

SFO **31.0%**

Weighted Average **21.9%**

N = 114 ultra-wealthy inheritors

Keeping in mind that many of the ultra-wealthy inheritors are strongly committed to becoming wealthier (see *Chapter 3: With Great Wealth Comes Great Responsibility*), it's not surprising that about 65% say they will become significantly involved in buying and selling substantial assets (Exhibit 7.2). Proportionately, nearly twice as many SFO ultra-wealthy inheritors see themselves moving in this direction compared to individual ultra-wealthy inheritors. Now, this anticipated involvement is not all about becoming wealthier, but it's often an essential element to extreme wealth creation.

EXHIBIT 7.2   Will Become Significantly More Involved in
Buying and Selling Substantial Assets

Individual	**41.9%**
SFO	**78.9%**
Weighted Average	**64.9%**

N = 114 ultra-wealthy inheritors

There are clear advantages for ultra-wealthy inheritors to directly invest in private companies or other assets including:

- Deepening of high-return profit sources.
- Leveraging their and their family's industry expertise.
- Capitalizing on their own and their family's relationships.
- Providing the opportunities to develop the vision and strategies of their investments.
- Offering the possibility of structuring the investments to be more tax efficient based tightly upon their own and their family's tax profile.

At the same time, there are obstacles to direct investing by the ultra-wealthy. The following are three well-noted obstacles:

- **Accessing high-quality investment opportunities.** Deal flow is a major consideration. Moreover, in this capacity the ultra-wealthy may very well be competing with the private equity funds and the investment banks for the "best" deals. Integral to the ultra-wealthy inheritors sourcing top-flight deals is their ability to leverage their extensive networks (see *Chapter 3: With Great Wealth Comes Great Responsibility; Chapter 13: Bargaining Brilliance; Chapter 14: Street-Smart Networking*).

- **Having the requisite professionals on tap to do the deals.** Ensuring the expertise is available—whether in-house or on an outsourced basis—is essential and potentially a serious problem. While there are a number of ways to identify and strongly motivate the requisite experts, we've not seen a great many of the ultra-wealthy systematically address this issue. The participatory compensation model (see *Chapter 20: The Family Office Solution*) is often the most effective way to employ the necessary talent and align interests.

- **Having family considerations derailing the investments**. Being involved in the strategy or management of the private companies, for example, can adversely complicate family matters. Furthermore, the success or failure of these investments may have repercussions for the family beyond the investors themselves. Consequently, making sure the family is aware and supportive of these efforts can be critical to making them work efficaciously.

Among ultra-wealthy inheritors who expect to be involved in the buying and selling of significant assets, most expect to be addressing the big picture issues such as strategy and vision. Another major function they're performing is sourcing opportunities (see above).

The importance of process expertise. In working with ultra-wealthy inheritors and the ultra-wealthy in general, we find that they periodically miss out on major opportunities. While these opportunities are bouncing around in their networks, their lack of a system-atized approach to managing their networks results in great deals being overlooked.

By developing the methodology to better capitalize on their outstanding relationships, we've seen ultra-wealthy inheritors markedly increase their deal-making prowess (see *Chapter 4: Enhancing Expertise; Chapter 13: Bargaining Brilliance; Chapter 14: Street-Smart Networking*). The ramifications for this are considerable to the extent ultra-wealthy inheritors are motivated to create private wealth.

In doing deals, being adept negotiators will prove critical. Again, we repeatedly see that the more agile and able ultra-wealthy negotiators are the ones who derive the greatest benefits. In a business context, they're the ones who fairly consistently garner the biggest paydays. What's also very telling is that the facile negotiators are usually able to apply their know-how across various industries. In effect, the ability to negotiate well super-sedes detailed industry knowledge in creating private wealth.

All in all, developing greater process expertise—an interest of many ultra-wealthy inheri-tors—is proven to be highly instrumental in their ability to profit doing deals. What is also quite evident is that the ultra-wealthy inheritors are not very interested in managing the technical aspects of a corporate acquisition or sale. Here, they'll often turn to high-caliber professionals. However, they'll usually want to understand the mechanics of the deal even if they don't get into all the details and nuances.

While deals take many forms, we see the appeal of club deals gaining considerable inter-est because of the obstacles noted coupled with a variety of other mitigating concerns.

THE RISE OF CLUB DEALS

Nearly 90% of the ultra-wealthy are highly interested in "club deals" (Exhibit 7.3). This is proportionately more the case for SFO ultra-wealthy inheritors.

Club deals are where the very wealthy co-invest in business ventures, real estate, and the like with other very wealthy individuals and families. In effect, the exceptionally affluent are getting together and forming a club to make investments, which are usually done on a deal by deal basis. A distinct advantage of many club deals is that they can be structured and managed by wealthy families often with the assistance of attorneys and investment bankers.

EXHIBIT 7.3 Highly Interested in "Club Deals"

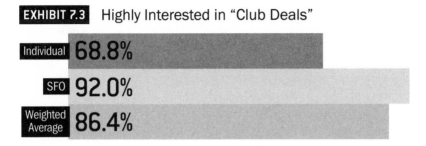

Individual	68.8%
SFO	92.0%
Weighted Average	86.4%

N = 114 ultra-wealthy inheritors

Often, to a meaningful degree, the obstacles we previously noted are diminished or might even completely fade away when doing club deals. Meanwhile, there are strategic advantages to well-constructed club deals such as not being locked into a projected return within an intended pre-set time frame, as is characteristic of private equity funds.

On the flip side, there is regularly an array of issues needing special attention when putting together club deals. Keep in mind that everyone is happy and supportive in the beginning. However, after the deal is closed there are likely to be more than a few speed bumps before profits are reaped. It's important for the success of these endeavors—on multiple levels—that the ultra-wealthy are embedded in the core processes driving results.

A major attraction of club deals frequently cited by the ultra-wealthy is their ability to capitalize on their personal and professional networks of other wealthy families and individuals. Here again we see the value and potential inherent in the relationships of the ultra-wealthy (see *Chapter 14: Street-Smart Networking*).

CONCLUSION
Direct investing in significant assets is or will be an important—and in some cases dominant— investment strategy for many ultra-wealthy inheritors. There are multiple reasons for this including an appreciation of the returns available coupled with a desire to distance themselves from intermediaries such as funds with their costs, performance, and liquidity issues.

One of the highest value resource ultra-wealthy inheritors bring to the process is their extensive and powerful networks. We've habitually found enormous high-quality business and investment opportunities embedded in the strong relationships of ultra-wealthy inheritors. While many of these opportunities are not always recognized, the focus of the ultra-wealthy on better leveraging their networks and their networking ability will likely result in a plethora of new high-quality investment possibilities.

Tied into the value of their networks, many ultra-wealthy inheritors are particularly interested in club deals. Here the monies of the exceptionally affluent are pooled. Moreover, for ultra-wealthy inheritors club deals can often provide various opportunities and advantages over other direct investing avenues.

8

CRITICAL
LIFESTYLE
SERVICES

IN THE WORLD OF THE ULTRA-WEALTHY,

moving beyond philanthropy and wealth management including deal making,
two sets of services tend to be in high demand. High quality healthcare is one.
Personal and family security is the other. Depending on circumstances, these two
sets of services can readily dominate the attention of the exceptionally affluent.

Ensuring the finest preventive medical care and treatments is something just about
everyone wants. The ultra-wealthy clearly have the resources to make this regularly
happen. At the same time, personal and family safety is generally a significant
matter and is often accentuated when the individuals involved are very well to do.

Let's begin by looking at healthcare.

HEALTHCARE

Nearly all the ultra-wealthy inheritors are highly interested in having ready access to top medical experts (Exhibit 8.1). The very wealthy are able to pay for the finest quality healthcare, which doesn't mean they always get the finest quality healthcare. The issue for them is to ensure that they are indeed dealing with the best medical professionals when their expertise is required.

EXHIBIT 8.1 Highly Interested in Having Access Top Medical Experts

Individual	**95.3%**
SFO	**95.8%**
Weighted Average	**95.6%**

N = 114 ultra-wealthy inheritors

Digging deeper, we find that a little more than eight out of ten strongly want to have access to top quality emergency healthcare anywhere and anytime (Exhibit 8.2). Irrespective of where they're traveling, their preference is to be able to source top-flight medical care. As many of the ultra-wealthy travel extensively (see *Chapter 1: Ultra-wealthy Inheritors*), the ability to have such expertise at their disposal whenever and wherever they might be in the world is particularly appealing.

Almost 70% are focused on being able to source medical experts for ongoing concerns. Continuous and attentive oversight, for example, of chronic illnesses is very important to many ultra-wealthy inheritors. Built into this is scrutiny of providers and second (third) opinions.

EXHIBIT 8.2 Concerned with Accessing High-Caliber Medical Care

INVOLVEMENT	INDIVIDUAL	SFO	WEIGHTED AVERAGE
Emergency healthcare anywhere at any time	81.4%	85.4%	83.3%
Ongoing medical concerns	69.8%	64.8%	66.7%

N = 114 ultra-wealthy inheritors

For the wealthy, and especially the ultra-wealthy, their motivation for top-of-the-line health-care coupled with the adverse complexities and complications of traditional healthcare systems leads many of them to concierge healthcare.

Concierge healthcare. The desire by the ultra-wealthy to have the ability to obtain the finest medical care for any reason whenever required is the reason for concierge health-care. A simple definition of concierge healthcare is that it's the *direct provisioning and/ or facilitation of medical care for a select membership.*

The big complication is that today concierge healthcare really takes many forms. On one end of the spectrum we have connected care including a direct relationship between a physician or physician group and a limited number of patients (see *Chapter 17: Connect-ed Care for the High-Net-Worth Family: Millennials Will Lead the Way*). At the other end of the spectrum, we have an oversight arrangement where the concierge healthcare organization acts as a coordinator and supervisor of medical care, but provides no medical care directly. Save for when the ultra-wealthy family exclusively employs a physician, concierge healthcare providers are membership organizations.

We're seeing that the decision to use the services of a concierge healthcare provider and, if so, which one, is predicated on two key factors. One factor—and the primary factor—is what the ultra-wealthy family is looking for to replace or augment their current medical providers. The other factor is the awareness of the ultra-wealthy concerning the concierge healthcare options.

There are quite a few very good concierge healthcare providers and more—both good and bad—are on the horizon. The ability to sift through all healthcare options and match up the best providers to their needs, wants, and preferences is a responsibility where 60% of the ultra-wealthy will likely become involved. Relatively more of the SFO ultra-wealthy inheritors are likely to be involved in the decision-making (Exhibit 8.3).

EXHIBIT 8.3 Will Become Significantly More Involved in Addressing Personal/Family Healthcare Resources

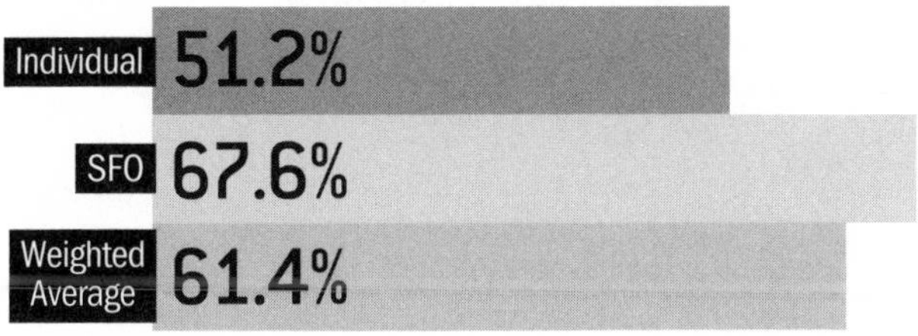

Individual **51.2%**

SFO **67.6%**

Weighted Average **61.4%**

N = 114 ultra-wealthy inheritors

Top-of-the-line healthcare tends to be a concern of everyone. Meanwhile, personal and family security is the other critical lifestyle service.

PERSONAL AND FAMILY SECURITY

As many ultra-wealthy inheritors look to take a more substantial role in selecting medical providers, the same is true of security providers (Exhibit 8.4). Almost 70% of them are likely to be taking the reins. The SFO ultra-wealthy inheritors are more inclined to become involved in personal and family security matters.

The decision to become more involved is very much a function of their concern about their own and their family's safety as well as the protection of their valuables. Moreover, they're also very concerned about the confidentiality of their professional and personal information.

EXHIBIT 8.4 Will Become Significantly More Involved in Addressing Family Security Resources

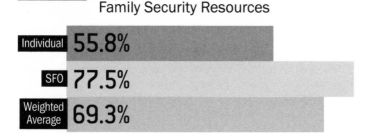

N = 114 ultra-wealthy inheritors

This isn't at all surprising considering the state of the world resulting in the wealthy having targets on their backs. Professional criminals, for example, will focus their nefarious efforts against the wealthy because of the potential returns considering the risks they're taking (see *Chapter 18: Combating Professional Criminals*).

Drilling down, we find that about 50% worry about predators, which is the most prevalent concern of the SFO ultra-wealthy inheritors (Exhibit 8.5). About two-fifths are concerned with potential robbery or muggings, and this is more common among the individual ultra-wealthy inheritors. Somewhat fewer are worried about acts of violence. Meanwhile, less than one-fifth of them are concerned about being abducted.

EXHIBIT 8.5 Very Important Personal and Family Protection Concerns

CONCERNS	INDIVIDUAL	SFO	WEIGHTED AVERAGE
Dealing with predators	41.9%	56.3%	50.9%
Potential robbery or muggings	48.8%	39.4%	43.0%
Acts of violence	37.2%	36.6%	36.8%
Potential abductions	18.6%	16.9%	17.5%

N = 114 ultra-wealthy inheritors

To address some of these concerns, the employment of close protection personnel is clearly on the rise. The ability to hire well-trained and experienced professionals to act as a barrier as well as deal with identified predators was once the domain of only the most affluent. Now those with considerable—but lesser—means are selectively utilizing these professionals to ensure their own safety as well as the safety of their loved ones. In a related vein, more and more of the very wealthy are looking to develop moderate proficiency in dealing with attackers (see *Chapter 19: Taking Matters Into Their Own Hands*).

One of the greatest concerns of nearly all ultra-wealthy inheritors is ensuring the confidentiality of personal and sensitive information (Exhibit 8.6). More than eight out of ten of them are concerned with SFO ultra-wealthy inheritors being proportionately more so. While there is a lot of angst over personal data, such as medical records and professional data such as proprietary deal terms being inappropriately shared, we find that relatively few ultra-wealthy individuals are taking adequate protective measures. There are a variety of steps—both human-based and technology-based—that would go a long way to ensuring privacy.

EXHIBIT 8.6 Very Concerned About Keeping Confidential Information Confidential

Individual	69.8%
SFO	91.5%
Weighted Average	83.3%

N = 114 ultra-wealthy inheritors

A comprehensive emergency response solution. A major need of many of the exceptionally affluent is the ability to address severe problematic situations immediately and forcefully. Examples of this include:

- Experiencing a disastrous car accident.

- Being trapped in a foreign country after a natural disaster.

- Dealing with an abduction.

- Needing emergency hospital care while vacationing.

- A stalker in another country aggressively taking action.

- Federal law enforcement knocking on the door.

About 80% of ultra-wealthy inheritors conclude it's very important to have comprehensive emergency response solutions (Exhibit 8.7). The issues here are the extent and breath of these solutions.

EXHIBIT 8.7 Very Important to Have Comprehensive Emergency Response Solutions

Individual	**76.7%**
SFO	**80.3%**
Weighted Average	**78.9%**

N = 114 ultra-wealthy inheritors

Considering that about half the ultra-wealthy inheritors travel extensively (see *Chapter 1: Ultra-Wealthy Inheritors*), today's comprehensive emergency response solution would regularly include:

- An on-site crisis management team.

- Immediate availability of legal and related expertise.

- Executive protection escort.

- 24/7/365 security emergency hotline.

- 24/7/365 emergency physician on-call.

- 24/7/365 connected care solution.

- Global evacuation service with oversight

- Global medevac service with oversight.

- Guaranteed foreign and specialist physician/hospital referral, care coordination and continuity.

- Guaranteed global security backup response.

- Personal medical kit.

- Archived personal medical records.

- Destination security/medical brief(s).

Clearly, this level of emergency responsiveness integrates the highest level of concierge healthcare with the highest level of family and personal security expertise. Moreover, the affluent client of this service should be provided with a smartphone app to call for help. The communications through the app will be encrypted. There would also be phone and computer based contact protocols as well.

CONCLUSION

Obtaining the finest medical care possible whenever they need it as well as dealing effectively and efficiently with an array of family and personal security matters always prove to be major concerns of the ultra-wealthy. This perspective is clearly seen among ultra-wealthy inheritors.

None of this should be surprising as most everyone would want these services. The big difference is that the ultra-wealthy are capable of affording them at the highest levels of competence. The connected care solution, for example, is a cost that not many people can manage. Similarly, the ability to develop and execute high-end strategies and tactics to ameliorate the threats imposed by professional criminals as well as respond to incidents offtimes requires substantial resources. Still, for the ultra-wealthy such lifestyle services are increasingly becoming normative.

While these sets of services don't come cheap, when they're needed, the ultra-wealthy rarely blink at the expense. This is certainly the case when it comes to comprehensive emergency response solutions.

CHAPTER
9

SELECTING
PROFESSIONAL
ADVISORS

THE KEY TO TACKLING the needs and wants of ultra-wealthy
inheritors is the network of professional advisors—the expert support structure—
that brings to the table state-of-the-art know-how and skills. Moreover, the ability
to orchestrate these experts on behalf of ultra-wealthy inheritors is essential. There
are a number of ways this function is accomplished from establishing family offices
(see *Chapter 20: The Family Office Solution*) to putting together a team of experts
under the direction of a designated or lead professional to the wealth creators or
scions taking charge of the processes.

An essential component to the effectiveness of this expert support structure is selecting the professional advisors involved. While it's quite common for most all professionals to laud their knowledge and abilities, relatively few of them are actually competent enough to adroitly deal with the requirements and demands of the ultra-wealthy. This has resulted in many of the ultra-wealthy inheritors and their families making mistakes in choosing professional advisors.

MISSTEPS

Ultra-wealthy inheritors are concerned with relying on professional advisors whose know-how and skills are not at the very top of their fields. From their own experiences and that of their family, friends, and business associates, there's the pervasive and dangerous situation where less than the best were hired. In fact, about three-quarters report members of their family or personally having hired less capable professional advisors than they should have (Exhibit 9.1). This was relatively more common among the individual ultra-wealthy inheritors.

EXHIBIT 9.1   Have Hired Less Capable Professional Advisors

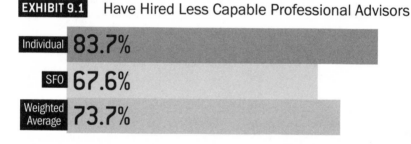

Individual 83.7%

SFO 67.6%

Weighted Average 73.7%

N = 114 ultra-wealthy inheritors

Some ultra-wealthy inheritors are quite adept at sourcing and managing professional advisors. At the same time, when ultra-wealthy inheritors, who are not presently adept, are educated on the processes that enable them to make better decisions in these contexts, their effectiveness at sourcing, selecting, and benefiting from professionals can increase exponentially (see *Chapter 4: Enhancing Expertise*). With a grasp of the fundamentals coupled with an understanding of how to identify and work with professional advisors (see below) augmented by an ability to capably negotiate (see *Chapter 13: Bargaining Brilliance*), many of these ultra-wealthy inheritors will be better able to effectively make wise selection decisions.

What's required of these experts is that they're not only among the best in their respective fields, but that they also exhibit the highest ethical and professional standards. What's very telling is that for little more than two-fifths of the ultra-wealthy inheritors, their family members or close friends and business associates have either been taken advantage of by professional advisors in their employ, or attempts have been made to do so, which proved ineffectual (Exhibit 9.2).

EXHIBIT 9.2   Taken Advantage of by Professional Advisors

Individual **46.5%**

SFO **42.3%**

Weighted Average **43.9%**

N = 114 ultra-wealthy inheritors

Essential to getting the best advice, services, and products is the ability to wisely identify the professional advisors with whom to work. This makes the astute selection of these authorities a critical function.

THE SELECTION PROCESS

Drawing on our respective work and experiences with the ultra-wealthy, combining the lessons learned from consulting with high-end professional services firms in conjunction with decades of research in the industry, we've delineated a systematic process to selecting remarkable professional advisors. What we're going to discuss are the very basic elements of this methodology in order to provide a fundamental overview. The supporting elements as well as the technical nuances have been intentionally ignored for instructional purposes.

Specification is the determination of the needs and wants, and—where possible—the nature of the expertise that will meet these preferences. It's where ultra-wealthy inheritors determine and specify, as clearly as possible, the goals and objectives for themselves and possibly their ultra-wealthy family.

Complications come from two directions. One is an inability to clearly define goals and objectives. This sometimes leads to a need to bring in expertise to help in this endeavor. The second complication is where the ultra-wealthy inheritors are unaware or unsure of the type of expertise they require and who can best provide it. Consequently, they're likely to turn to others for the answers. As such, the first two phases of the selection process—specification and identification—are often tightly entwined.

Identification is the development of a short list of potential professional advisors, who are capable of delivering extraordinarily high-quality services and products that meet the stipulated agenda of ultra-wealthy inheritors. There are a number of ways to do this, and most of the ultra-wealthy employ a variety of approaches. Nevertheless, most times prospective professional advisors are identified by referral (Exhibit 9.3).

For almost eight out of ten, referrals from trusted professional advisors are the way ultra-wealthy inheritors regularly access other high-caliber experts. It's the number one method for all ultra-wealthy inheritors and is more prevalent among the SFO ultra-wealthy inheritors.

The reasons for this are fairly straightforward. The professional advisors who the ultra-wealthy are currently engaging are inclined to know other experts who have the knowledge and skills to adroitly address the matters in question. What's important in this scenario is that the ultra-wealthy inheritors are keenly aware of the nature of the relationship between the referring professional advisor and the experts he or she recommends (see below).

Next in overall importance is the research they themselves conduct to identify high-caliber professional advisors. This is done by more than one-third of them with the SFO ultra-wealthy inheritors more likely to conduct their own research.

For 35% of the ultra-wealthy inheritors, their peers play a critical role in identifying industry authorities to hire. Half the individual ultra-wealthy inheritors look to their peers while a quarter of the SFO ultra-wealthy inheritors turn to their peers. As many of them are highly networked—increasingly with each other—ultra-wealthy inheritors have experiences with professionals who they're very willing to share (see *Chapter 4: Enhancing Expertise*). They're looking to evaluate whom someone else employed and the outcomes or ongoing results they attained.

A little more than one-fifth of the respondents report that they find professional advisors by consulting with various single-family offices. Understandably, this is much more prevalent among the SFO ultra-wealthy inheritors. More than ever, single-family offices are highly professionally/personally interconnected and are turning to each other for recommendations on what professional advisors to engage as well as in determining best practices.

One-fifth turn to family members to find professional advisors, and individual ultra-wealthy inheritors dominate this percentage. Very often these family members are from their own cohort as opposed to an older generation. Sometimes the experiences they've had with their parent's experts, for instance, has been less than rewarding. This leads them to look elsewhere. In effect, these family members are peers.

Only two of the ultra-wealthy inheritors said they respond to unsolicited advances by professional advisors. The idea of a professional advisor getting a list of ultra-wealthy inheritors and thinking that clients would come from cold calling this list is usually a big mistake. While there are certainly times ultra-wealthy inheritors will respond to an unsolicited approach, this is the exception as opposed to the rule.

EXHIBIT 9.3 Likely Ways to Find a Professional

SOURCE	INDIVIDUAL	SFO	WEIGHTED AVERAGE
Referrals from trusted professionals	60.5%	90.1%	78.9%
Personal research in the field	25.6%	42.3%	36.0%
Referrals from peers	51.2%	25.4%	35.1%
Referrals from other SFOs	2.3%	35.2%	22.8%
Referrals from family members	39.5%	8.5%	20.2%
Unsolicited approach by the professional	4.7%	0.0%	1.8%

N = 114 ultra-wealthy inheritors

What's evident is that ultra-wealthy inheritors like most of the exceptionally affluent turn to knowing individuals—other professional advisors—in order to identify leading authorities whose expertise they require. Unlike most of the self-made ultra-wealthy, many of the ultra-wealthy inheritors will look for advice in this regard from their peers, who might be family members or not. While peers tend to make referrals based on corollary situations and their experiences with various experts, professional advisors often incorporate other factors. For example, most professional advisors are inclined to introduce their ultra-wealthy clients to other professional advisors who are thought leaders.

Thought leaders are recognized industry authorities. They're the professional advisors their peers acknowledge as being the foremost specialists in their respective fields. Thought leaders are acknowledged by industry authorities to be savants. In effect, they're certainly some of the very best at what they do.

The decision by professional advisors to refer other professional advisors who are thought leaders is a risk-reduction strategy. By recommending a renowned expert in another field, a professional advisor is mitigating the possibility of something going amiss, which would only prove disadvantageous to all involved. It's important to note that if a professional advisor is unable to direct an ultra-wealthy individual to a high-caliber expert in another field, there's the real question of the competency and industry connectivity of that individual.

For the ultra-wealthy, thought leadership can be a critical deciding factor in the professional advisors they employ. As professional advisors recognize the importance of thought leadership, the bar to become a thought leader continues to rise. We're finding that the exceptionally affluent are more than ever choosing to work with professional advisors who are truly moving their respective industries forwards. For the ultra-wealthy, it's all about being able to access the smartest and the brightest whenever possible.

In addition to being thought leaders, or better yet, "knowledge entrepreneurs," there are a number of additional related criteria being extensively employed by the ultra-wealthy when selecting professionals. Included here are:

- **Transparency.** Everything is readily explained and disclosed. At no time is there any attempt at obfuscation or engagement in clever subtlety. For example, the fee structures charged to ultra-wealthy inheritors are communicated clearly and precisely (see below).

- **No hidden or additional agendas.** The motivations of the professional advisors are manifest. They're always openly noted; they're made obvious. Any potential conflicts or non-aligned preferences are readily disclosed and discoursed.

- **Open and regular communications.** A steady stream of information back and forth is optimal and usually essential to an on-going viable relationship. This includes, but goes beyond scheduled meetings and other forms of communications. While Internet-based communications have a place for the purposes of high-consequence communications, in-person meetings are often preferred.

- **Full disclosure of compensation arrangements.** The nature and level of compensation is made explicit. The fees and commissions that are imbedded in products are detailed. Because of the complexity of some of the offerings or the characteristics of the professional services (e.g., legal work), it's important to clinically breakdown the cost structure. "Cost surprises" are to be avoided at all costs.

Once professional advisors are identified, the next step is to evaluate them. In part, based on the way they were sourced, a degree of verification has already been done. For example, if another professional advisor made the introduction, the ultra-wealthy inheritor is depending on the referring party to have conducted a careful evaluation of the qualities, personal characteristics, and capabilities of the expert. Still, it's ofttimes very wise to conduct an independent screening of the prospective professional advisor hire.

Due diligence is a careful and intense screening of potential professional advisors. Ideally, all potential providers need to be carefully vetted. Unfortunately, the quality of the due diligence process is many times questionable.

The level of due diligence varies extensively based on many factors. Included here are:

- The way the professional advisor was first sourced.
- The prospective level of access to the ultra-wealthy inheritor.
- The amount and nature of the confidential information the professional advisor requires in order to be effective.

- The time frame within which the analysis must be conducted.
- The criticality of the expertise provided by the professional advisor.

A wide variety of issues need to be considered when evaluating the credibility of professional advisors. When the expertise required is highly critical, an inclusive background assessment as well as a detailed current analysis is regularly called for. This is the same type of investigatory expertise that is used against professional criminals (see *Chapter 18: Combating Professional Criminals*). Providing the expert passes the background investigation, it's time to negotiate the arrangement.

Negotiation is about taking the short-list of professional advisors (or the individual professional advisor chosen) and bargaining with them over the precise terms of the engagement. We've found a greater tendency for negotiating on these matters to be pretty much second nature for extreme wealth creators, but it's not always the approach taken by ultra-wealthy inheritors. It's very important for ultra-wealthy inheritors to negotiate so as to get the best "arrangement" possible.

The negotiation should address a number of broadly conceptualized issues. The following are examples with questions needing to be considered:

THE DELIVERABLES.

- What know-how and products are the professional advisors providing and why?
- How are results to be evaluated?
- What are the time frames for receiving the deliverables?

THE COST OF THE DELIVERABLES.

- How are the costs for specialized knowledge and products determined?
- Where can expenses be rationalized?
- What is the pecuniary relationship between cost and value?

OPERATING RELATIONSHIP.

- How is the process of providing the deliverables going to work?
- How are exceptions going to be handled?
- What is the nature of the ongoing relationship?

What's critical to recognize is that—at this level of wealth and professionalism—many deliverables are bespoke, so core aspects and elements can consequently be negotiated.

The ability to skillfully negotiate (see *Chapter 13: Bargaining Brilliance*) is usually significant in enabling ultra-wealthy inheritors to get maximum value. It's quite common for the ultra-wealthy to come out of these kinds of negotiations—provided they are adept bargainers—with a 200% to 500% increase in value to cost.

Engagement is where the agreed parameters of the relationship between the professional advisor and the ultra-wealthy inheritor are contracted. Now there's a clear description of deliverables as well as the parameters of the ongoing working relationship.

CONCLUSION

Without question, ultra-wealthy inheritors are taking the reins. From philanthropy to choosing money managers to doing deals, many are becoming more involved in critical decision-making. Indispensable to their effectiveness and long-term success is their ability to select high-caliber professional advisors with whom to work.

Many, having had negative experiences with professional advisors, are more astute and process-oriented in identifying and deciding whom to employ. The selection process detailed here explains the critical phases that are often needed in order to make intelligent and informed decisions. While not a panacea, this process or similar ones can be very fruitful by ensuring ultra-wealthy inheritors are able to acquire cost-effectively the high-caliber expertise they want.

At the same time, ultra-wealthy inheritors are likely to become ever more adept and, consequently, more discriminating as they expand their own activities including making better use of their usually extensive and influential networks. Education on the best practices in sourcing professional advisors refined by experience will produce very astute purchasers of high-caliber professional services and products.

PART III
Expert Perspectives

10

HELPING WEALTHY INHERITORS CHANGE THE WORLD

by Jonah Wittkamper

FOR MANY WEALTHY INHERITORS, philanthropy plays a central role in their lives (see *Chapter 5: Philanthropy*). It's often a function of their upbringing (see *Chapter 2: Inheriting More Than Money*) as well as their own sensibilities. Making a significant positive change in the world is often characteristic of these individuals (see *Chapter 3: With Great Wealth Comes Great Responsibility*) with charitable endeavors having a pivotal role.

At the same time, their thinking and approach to philanthropy is evolving in powerful and meaningful ways. They appreciate and use technology; they work to ensure that their philanthropic actions deliver measurable results; they focus more and more on social entrepreneurship. These patterns illustrate their perspective and drive to make a difference, and increasingly define them as a generation.

SOCIAL ENTREPRENEURSHIP

If business entrepreneurship is the innovation of the marketplace to meet unmet needs or to achieve business needs in more effective ways, then social entrepreneurship is the equivalent in the social sphere. It's characterized, on the one hand, by non-profit ventures that address root causes and generate income for sustainability, and on the other hand, by for-profit companies that generate profits as well as social and environmental returns.

There's a spectrum from ventures that prioritize addressing social issues above all else to ventures that prioritize generating profit above all else. It's important to note that social entrepreneurship differs from corporate social responsibility with which it's sometimes confused.

- Social entrepreneurship is about innovation: doing things in new ways, tackling unmet needs, re-using resources creatively.
- Social entrepreneurship is about the entrepreneurial spirit: taking risks, refusing to give up, obsessing about solutions until they are found, creating new "things" and bringing them to scale.

What is clear is that there are quite a number of wealthy inheritors who have embraced the concept, philosophy, and logic of social entrepreneurship. What is also evident is that there's a gap between the desire to do something and doing something well and at scale. The Nexus Global Youth Summit (www.nexusyouthsummit.org) was created to bridge the gap.

CONNECTING AND EDUCATING INHERITORS

Nexus is a global platform designed to connect and unite the millennial generation in order to address global problems in three primary ways:

- To serve as a bridge between communities of wealth and social entrepreneurship.
- To advance the potential and influence of young people across lines of industry, expertise, partisanship, race, nationality, religion, etc.
- To increase and improve both philanthropy and social impact investing.

As of late 2013, Nexus enjoys a membership of more than 2,000 members from over 70 countries. They include leading young social entrepreneurs and young inheritors from hundreds of the world's influential business families.

Nexus is proving to be a magnet for the millennial generation. Most Nexus members have extra financial resources or will someday, and are seeking the latest ideas in social innovation and impact investing (see *Chapter 6: Wealth Management*). The organization provides a safe yet inclusive space. Young social entrepreneurs and allies, who understand and support the social and emotional challenges of wealth-holders, may be invited to participate, share their expertise, and develop relationships. Central to the power of Nexus is the focus on community and alliance building.

The key is collaboration. The primary value of Nexus is its membership. The members bring expertise and resources to the table as well as the desire to work together. Nexus members collaborate in many ways:

- They hire each other.

- They join each other's boards.

- They fund each other's projects.

- They help redesign each other's companies and organizations.

- They brainstorm new social movements and create new possibilities and outcomes together that were never possible before.

While Nexus is a relatively new organization, there are many examples of members collaborating and getting results. For instance, Nexus members were instrumental in a creating a company called Constellation. The most common form of cancer is skin cancer. It's also the most treatable when detected early. The best way to catch skin cancer is to examine and track the moles on your skin. Constellation is a health-tech start-up that is developing a full body scan to monitor and track your moles. This way a person's entire body is completely and carefully examined enabling you to see any changes in your moles over time and identify irregularities. See www.constellation.io

Another example is Satisfeito, which is a global movement to help eliminate child hunger while preventing food waste at restaurants. Conceived at Nexus and later implemented in Sao Paulo, Brazil, it is spreading. Restaurants modify their menus to allow customers to order smaller portions. Less food is consumed and the money saved goes to non-profits that feed children. See www.satisfeito.com

There are many other examples of collaboration as well including the PVBLIC Foundation (a system for donating unused media assets to non-profits—www.pvblic.org), Just Good (a healthy life style movement and aggregator of social good products—www.justgood.org), Good Super (Australia's first social impact retirement fund—www.goodsuper.com.au), the Common Ground Donor Network (an alliance of conservative and progressive philanthropists seeking common ground on policy—www.cgdn.us), the Association of Global Conveners (an effort to promote collaboration among conference leaders—www.conveners.org), the Global Campaign for a Culture of Philanthropy (a movement to pass a UN resolution on promoting philanthropy), investments in various social startups, and much more.

The Nexus Summits. The thriving center of Nexus is the Global Summit, together with the many regional Summits that feed into it. The best way to understand the magic of Nexus is to picture the United Nations. Picture the inspiration that comes from meeting people from dozens of countries. Picture the ability to help bring ideas into action because people with talent and resources are at the table and eager to work with each other. This is Nexus. It is a movement that bridges communities of wealth and social entrepreneurship by hosting summits both at the United Nations in New York and in major cities all over the world.

Through keynote speeches, panel discussions, and expert led dialogues as well as informal meals, one-on-one sessions, and online forums, Nexus offers a wide array of educational and experiential learning opportunities as well as an amazing community of people for once-in-a-life-time quality connections and collaborations.

The process helps wealthy inheritors and social entrepreneurs to connect, learn from each other, and do great things. This is the objective of Nexus, and the methodologies that foster creativity and action are core to organization.

MEETING DEMAND

Currently, nearly a dozen financial and professional services institutions organize delegations of their top clients (and potential clients) to Nexus. And, the number is growing. The organization is quickly becoming the leading program for educating next generation wealth-holders and young business leaders about impact investing, philanthropy, and responsible leadership.

The organization is growing exponentially and speculates that in the next three years it will play a significant role within a majority of the families on the Forbes wealth lists as well as a majority of the top banks and other leading service providers to the ultra-wealthy. Part of this expansion will happen by design, and part will happen in response to the demand from the organization's constituencies.

Some financial institutions engage Nexus to help develop and expand their own internal programming for nextgen wealth-holders. Currently, there are Nexus teams in about twenty countries who are planning to host Summits in their largest cities. As noted, the organization has summits in every major region of the world. The partnership with the United Nations is also growing, and more regional collaboration is expected there, as well.

As Nexus' global footprint expands, there's the need to develop greater local programming as well. Local programs include: Salon dinners for members of the network to explore key issues and build relationships; leadership development retreats to foster greater personal awareness, self-identity, management abilities, and more; tours and site visits to organizations, foundations, and social impact businesses around the world.

Beyond improving, increasing, and diversifying its programming at local levels, the group is designing partnerships with numerous governmental and multi-lateral agencies to help organize the influence of young people in those institutions and to push the envelope on public-private partnerships.

CONCLUSION

In the world of ultra-wealthy inheritors, Nexus is filling a burgeoning need. There are a large and growing number of wealth-holders who are highly committed to making the world better for everyone. They have embraced social entrepreneurship, and Nexus provides the foremost global platform to learn from peers and practitioners, develop relationships, and explore new ventures.

It is a challenge for the organization to meet the growing demands and expectations of its constituents, but it will be possible by partnering with key organizations and individuals throughout the world who can help to steward the network and develop extreme depth of expertise in how to change the world.

Jonah Wittkamper is the Co-Founder and Global Director of the Nexus Global Youth Summit (www.nexusyouthsummit.org), a network of young wealth-holders and social entrepreneurs. He has organized global networks of young philanthropists for nearly a decade, inspiring new charitable activity from many of the world's wealthiest families. Prior to Nexus, Jonah helped build the text messaging platform of the Obama campaign, founded two technology startups, led the US domestic program of Search for Common Ground, and co-founded the Global Youth Action Network/TakingITGlobal.org, the largest online community of young social change leaders and youth-focused non-profit organizations. Currently based in Washington, DC, he has lived in Brazil, speaks three languages, and is a proud graduate of Camp Rising Sun and Williams College.

THE EDUCATION OF
GLOBAL STEWARDS

by Russ Alan Prince & Hannah Shaw Grove

THERE ARE SIGNIFICANT INTERRELATED SOCIETAL,

environmental, health, and economic issues that need to be addressed in order
to ensure a prosperous future for the Earth's inhabitants. To be successful in
thoughtfully and effectively dealing with these issues requires the collaboration
and support of many types of institutions. In this mix of cooperating organizations
and people, we have "education."

Education takes many forms and has become fundamental to successfully
managing and leading in today's complex, increasingly transparent, hyper-
competitive commercial landscape. It's also proving instrumental in all aspects
of creating effectual governmental and non-profit organizations.

While the adoption of high-caliber education is becoming ubiquitous, the future ability of educational programs to meaningfully empower people, to tackle pressing and decisive issues, today and tomorrow, will need to continually evolve. Many extremely successful and provably capable people are recognizing the perpetual and escalating changes they need to adroitly deal with in order to maintain, let alone boost, the success of the enterprises they're involved with as well as their personal accomplishments. This is translating into these individuals embracing life long learning.

Personal development—in its many manifestations—enables people to achieve success as well as provide the means to reach ever-higher levels of achievement. Education that's transformative, issues-focused, and emphasizes reflective awareness is what successful people, who are looking to make greater advances including personal triumphs, are looking for.

There's also a profound shift in the way many of these successful individuals, as well as those fast-tracking to higher levels of accomplishment, will choose to learn in addition to the way they're going to choose the curriculum they pursue. The trend is solidly to a much more customized, transdisciplinary action-oriented educational experience.

Another trend that's coalescing is the critical importance of global stewardship.

THE PRESENT AND FUTURE IN THE HANDS OF GLOBAL STEWARDS

Many people talk about the need for global leaders. They're positing the world's requirement for individuals who can organize and motivate others for a common goal. As for the leaders being "global," this entails their ability to influence other people taking into account the internationalization of business and philanthropy as well as the impact of a highly connected world that we all experience no matter where we're located. In many respects, quite a number of business schools, consultancies, think tanks, and training organizations are indeed focused on providing the educational foundation global leaders require in order to become more effective.

Educating global leaders, however, falls short of what is becoming necessary to not only garner exceptional business success, but to also create maximum wealth on every level—worldwide, regional, country, local, and personal. For wealth to be created on all these levels, global leaders may not be enough. The answer may very well be **global stewards**.

This is accomplished by providing the means to deftly combine educating global leaders with a strong understanding, facility, and appropriate skills for thoughtful stewardship. Global stewards are leaders complemented with sensitized professional judgment derived from knowledge, skills, values, and ethics.

Stewardship is a mind-set supported by select skills that's centered on the responsible and conscientious management of resources. Having the appropriate mental perspectives and insights to be a steward is not enough. What are also required are the skills and competencies to be effective.

Accepting responsibility, for example, is a core characteristic of global stewards. In addition, accountability is an undisputed given in the world of global stewards. This is made all the more complicated by the multiple constituencies the global steward must connect and work with in order to garner meaningful results.

The simplified framework for global stewardship starts with entrepreneurial capitalism (Exhibit 11.1). This precept embodies numerous attributes that result in business-related success such as creativity, productive competitiveness, resourcefulness, and measurable results. Two key consequences of entrepreneurial capitalism are sustainability and world-wide wealth creation.

EXHIBIT 11.1   A Core Framework for Global Stewardship

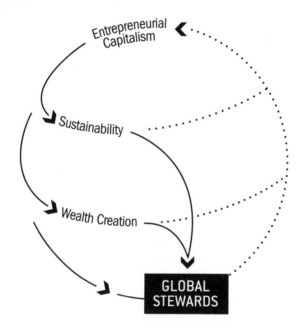

Sustainability is the ability to last. It's the careful and wise husbanding and magnification of resources to produce maximum benefit while making certain requisite resources are available in the future. The singularly focused, mindless pursuit of profit will not produce the long lasting and needed results we all need to enhance the lives of all the people on the planet as well as every other living creature.

To the extent possible, people need to look and consider all interactions among business, government, non-profits, the environment, and society. This doesn't negate the need to create wealth, but it does set parameters on what actions are viable and acceptable.

While pursuing sustainability, entrepreneurial capitalism is also very tightly focused on significant **wealth creation**. As noted, the intent is to create wealth on every level. At the corporate level, for example, the need to be strategically innovative can be instrumental in the success of the business and all involved. This is the embodiment of constructive achievement. The ability for everyone to become seriously wealthier certainly has the potential to transform the world for the better.

By focusing on sustainable growth in conjunction with universal wealth creation, a potent set of relationships is established. What can and hopefully will evolve is a virtuous cycle where all the components reinforce each other. Ultimately, the end-goal is to make a better and more prosperous world for everyone.

This lofty goal doesn't negate the fact that trade-offs and hard choices need to be made. What global stewards do is look for solutions incorporating well-reasoned and inclusive thinking. Critically, global stewards are global leaders possessing moral depth, ingenuity, and cognitive sophistication in the service of the planet, writ large.

Helping educate global stewards is arduous and essential. The pedagogical mechanics have to center on clearly articulating and actualizing professional (and often personal) development of those aspiring to become or better themselves as global stewards.

FOSTERING CAPABLE

The requisite educational approach is geared intently around facilitating achievements. The focus of any viable educational program is to provide extraordinary and highly actionable curriculum that will enable people to excel. It's the very no-nonsense approach global stewards, as well as those seeking to fast-track to greater accomplishments, demand.

Global stewards are results driven, and consequently, their education must also be results proven. Today, it's not just aspiring global stewards who require being able to deliver discernable consequential results. This is the standard for all individuals wanting to better themselves professionally. Time is a cost few can squander. Education has to translate into accomplishments as fast as reasonably possible.

Theory, for instance, is nice and can certainly play a very important role in a person's professional development. Theory can deliver insights and be effective in identifying opportunities and possibilities. But for global stewards, theory alone is often quite limited and insufficient. For theory to have maximum value in today's highly complicated and convoluted world, it must provide guidelines and backing for action. Thus, learning various theories without learning how to apply them is not as productive as possible. What global stewards require is for theories to be tightly bound with competencies.

The following equation lays out the nature of the education global stewards and what all those looking to professionally excel require:

$$\text{Applicable} + \text{Practical} = \textbf{CAPABLE}$$

Let's consider each of the components:

- **Applicable.** The educational content must be pertinent, relevant, and exceedingly appropriate to the issues, resources, and situations global stewards and others are facing or will face. Hence, there must be foundational material and more targeted content as part of a customizable curriculum such as issue-oriented material.

- **Practical.** The educational content must prepare people to efficaciously handle complex and conflict ridden important matters as well as enable them to take on the mantle of stewardship. Furthermore, the educational content, where possible, should promote creativity and constructive cleverness. The world is dynamically changing requiring that people quickly and meritoriously adapt.

- **Capable.** By adroitly ensuring the curriculum is *applicable* and *practical*, dedicated individuals exit quite capable. They will have the knowledge and skills, the insights and proficiencies, to more efficaciously achieve high degrees of success. They will be able to make a significant difference in their professional lives and in whatever endeavors they pursue.

IMPLICATIONS FOR ULTRA-WEALTHY INHERITORS

As shown in *Chapter 3: With Great Wealth Comes Great Responsibility*, most of those surveyed desire to do something significant in the world. Included here is a desire to achieve their professional goals as well as having a keen interest in philanthropy, especially social entrepreneurship. At the same time, ultra-wealthy inheritors recognize areas where they can increase their skills and knowledge (see *Chapter 4: Enhancing Expertise*).

In taking the reins, ultra-wealthy inheritors are very likely to have a dramatic and far reaching impact on many facets of the lives and well-being of all living things throughout the world. They are especially well positioned because of their upbringing, wealth, and commitments to take on the role of global stewards (see *Coda: Seven Trends Changing the World of Ultra-Wealthy Inheritors*).

While some ultra-wealthy inheritors will be more than able to become global stewards based on their present positioning, expertise, and abilities, others will look to enhance their knowledge, skills, capabilities, and perceptions. They will then turn to educational resources that are highly adaptable and designed to meet their needs, wants, and preferences on multiple levels. Education, as described, is one of the contributing ways a percentage of ultra-wealthy inheritors will transition to becoming or heighten their capacity to be global stewards.

Hannah Shaw Grove (www.hsgrove.com) is one of the world's leading experts on private wealth and family offices. Her reputation was built on more than 20 years of hands-on work with wealthy families and the professionals they rely on for key financial and lifestyle services, complemented by extensive statistical research with the same constituencies. She is the author of ten books and dozens of reports and articles that represent her empirical, theoretical and anecdotal findings, and a founder of Private Wealth *magazine. Ms. Grove consults to the world's wealthiest families and their closest advisors on the creation and operation of family offices.*

CHAPTER

12

ULTRA-WEALTHY
CONNOISSEURS

by Douglas D. Gollan & Russ Alan Prince

A VERY SMALL BUT INCREDIBLY influential group among the ultra-wealthy is connoisseur collectors. Their importance is a function of their authority and impact in their respective fields of interest such as artwork, watches, coins, and wines. Furthermore, they're likely to also have significant influence on the high-end luxury products and services preferences of the wealthy as well as those aspiring to greater affluence.

What's also evident is that these exceptionally well-to-do individuals are not only reflecting tastes, but are offtimes contributory to the tastes especially among the mass collector culture as well as passion investors (of which they're not; see below). Their influence is derived from their commitment to developing a deep understanding of their field of interest coupled with their willingness to use their monies in "perfecting" their collections.

THREE SEGMENTS

To better understand ultra-wealthy connoisseurs, let's divide those who create substantial and valuable collections into three segments (Exhibit 12.1):

- **Cubs** are ultra-wealthy with limited quality collecting experience and expertise. They're comparative beginners exploring a field of interest with the prospects of one day managing and enhancing or starting a collection of note.

- **Collectors** are ultra-wealthy, who through immersion or because of a personal proclivity, have created or are managing a valuable collection. Relatively speaking, they're educated and experienced in their field of interest. However, they're not nearly as erudite in their field of interest as the next segment.

- **Connoisseurs** are at the intellectual pinnacle of their field of interest. They're established experts in their own right and complementarily quite experienced. They're exceedingly adept and dedicated to not only perfect their collection, but also mastery of their field of interest.

EXHIBIT 12.1 Three Segments

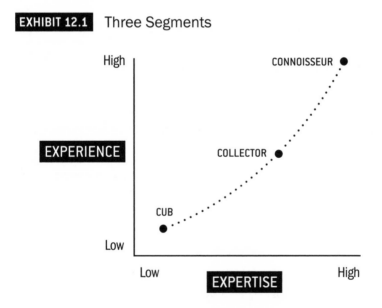

While far from scientific, based solely on our dealing with the ultra-wealthy, we guestimate that Collectors make up the majority and are somewhere in the range of 60% to 70% of this population (Exhibit 12.2). Cubs account for something like 30% to 40% of this population. Thus, true Connoisseurs only constitute, at the far outside, 5% of the ultra-wealthy who are building or managing meaningful, substantial collections. However, the psychology of Connoisseurs is most informative as it shines a spotlight on key, often obscure corners of the mindset, thinking, and actions of the rich and super-rich.

EXHIBIT 12.2

Segment Percentage Estimates

N = 114 ultra-wealthy inheritors

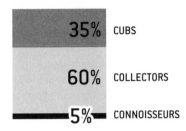

35% CUBS

60% COLLECTORS

5% CONNOISSEURS

Before addressing some critical aspects of Connoisseurs, it's worthwhile to note that many of the ultra-wealthy collect. This was evidenced in the survey of ultra-wealthy inheritors.

COLLECTING BY ULTRA-WEALTHY INHERITORS AND THEIR FAMILIES

Nearly 70% of the ultra-wealthy inheritors have a collection of some kind in their families. This includes their personal collections (Exhibit 12.3).

EXHIBIT 12.3 Have a Family or Personal Collection

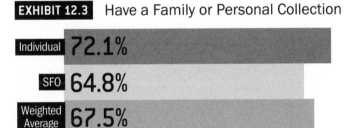

Individual **72.1%**

SFO **64.8%**

Weighted Average **67.5%**

N = 114 ultra-wealthy inheritors

The following are the main types of collections these ultra-wealthy families have reported assembling:

FINE ART	RARE BOOKS & MANUSCRIPTS
WINE & SPIRITS	COINS & STAMPS
JEWELS & JEWELRY	ANTIQUES
WATCHES	RARE RUGS
CARS & VINTAGE AIRCRAFT	PHOTOGRAPHS & FILMS

It's also important to note that four of the 114 survey respondents specified their families established museums. They were constructed to house their own collections as well as related works.

What's evident is that a sizable percentage of these ultra-wealthy inheritors or their families are engaged in collecting. In all probability we would define them as Collectors as opposed to Cubs or Connoisseurs. Still, a portion of them might fit into these other two segments. What's proving more informative—and characteristic of ultra-wealthy inheritors—is their motivation to take a decision-making role concerning their collections (see below).

With greater involvement in creating, building, and managing significant collections, we anticipate a strong increase in the relative percentage of ultra-wealthy inheritors becoming Connoisseurs. This will, in turn, meaningfully affect their fields of interest as well as have positive repercussions for the luxury industry and society. So, before addressing ultra-wealthy inheritors taking the reins, we first turn our attention to the nature of exceptionally affluent Connoisseurs starting with ameliorating some misperceptions.

CORRECTING TWO POINTS OF CONFUSION

A good place to begin is what ultra-wealthy Connoisseurs are NOT as we commonly find some misunderstandings. Simply put, ultra-wealthy Connoisseurs are not passion investors, nor are they ruled by their emotions.

Passion investing is where the affluent invest in luxury items with the expectation of these items appreciating coupled with the intention of making a profit on their sale (Exhibit 12.4). To a great extent it's about investing, first and foremost, in the asset class (broadly defined) as "luxury." For many passion investors, there's the appeal of the luxury items; however, their fascination and appreciation of these items pales compared to that of the Connoisseur.

Passion investors are looking for assets that will increase in value. While investing in coins, for example, their level of expertise in numismatics tends to be limited. In contrast, Connoisseurs are—by definition—expert and accomplished in their field of interest.

Whereas the passion investor intends to sell the collection at a future date, the Connoisseur is very much less inclined. With the preference to keep the collection intact, Connoisseurs are motivated to maintain them in their lifetimes, and either transfer the collection to future generations or to appropriate charitable organizations such as museums. When Connoisseurs sell their prized collections, it's commonly under duress such as in cases of bankruptcy or divorce.

EXHIBIT 12.4 Passion Investors and Connoisseurs

CHARACTERISTICS	PASSION INVESTORS	CONNOISSEURS
Investment quality primary importance	Yes	No
Field expertise	Rarely or often limited	By definition
Intent on selling at a future date	Yes	Preferably not

Compulsive behavior is sometimes mistakenly attributed to Connoisseurs. This is far from reality. The difference between being a Connoisseur and a fixated eccentric depends in part on whether other, more important aspects of life are neglected. It's not uncommon for compulsive collectors to get so immersed in their obsessions that their professional and personal lives suffer. For Connoisseurs, building a significant collection is but one facet—albeit often an important facet—of their lives.

In addition, the role of emotional decision-making while characteristic of fixated eccentrics is not typical of Connoisseurs who are habitually anything but impulsive. Acquisition decisions are exceedingly rational and well thought through. Their expertise in their field of interest provides them with the requisite knowledge and insights to make highly informed calculated choices.

Along the same lines, whereas compulsive collectors are known to lose astute decision-making capabilities (presuming they had such abilities to start) in many acquisition scenarios, Connoisseurs are known for their precision and exactitude. While highly passionate when it comes to their field of interest, their desires don't distract them cerebrally.

Having briefly addressed what ultra-wealthy Connoisseurs are not, we turn to the core psychological factors that motivate them.

PSYCHOLOGICAL PERSPECTIVES

When it comes to expert collecting—the world of Connoisseurs—we find three sets of interrelated psychological factors in play (Exhibit 12.5). There's the creation of identity; there's the sense of evolved well-being; there's the pursuit of "absolute" mastery of the field of interest.

EXHIBIT 12.5 Psychological Perspectives

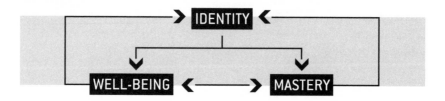

Identity encompasses the Connoisseur's sense of self in relation to the process and result of building a prestigious collection. It's the manifestation of ego fueled by demonstrable accomplishments. The collection regularly will be a manifestation of the unique aspects of the Connoisseur. It's a powerful form of self-expression and self-extension.

There's little doubt that Connoisseurs see themselves in their collections as they see themselves in other activities that are extremely meaningful to them such as business and philanthropy. For these elite collectors, their collections are deep reflections of themselves, and in this way, they impact decision-making across a spectrum of personal and professional issues.

Evolved well-being entails the progressive feelings of happiness derived from expanding and managing a top-flight collection. Connoisseurs are passionate when it comes to their collections. These feelings can sometimes rival the ardent attachments people have for loved ones.

The evolved well-being comes from "being one" with the process of collecting and the collection itself. Often this is referred to as "flow," which is where the Connoisseur becomes so intensely immersed in aspects of acquisition or the collection per se that the experience is extraordinarily pleasurable.

Pursuit of mastery includes all components where Connoisseurs become expert (i.e., extremely knowledgeable and insightful) in their field of interest. At this point, their high-level mental skill proficiencies are evidenced in:

• Their ability to observe acutely.

• Their capacity to rapidly and fluidly make fine distinctions and comparisons.

• Their facility at recognizing patterns within their collection including not only the elements that make up the collection, but the gaps in it as well.

Ultra-wealthy connoisseurs have learned their fields of interest through hard work coupled with leveraging their talents and desires. Their monies contributed tremendously by enabling them to work with and deal with professionals and other connoisseurs as well as provided the means to actively invest in their field of interest.

Many ultra-wealthy inheritors are motivated to take control or be very influential when it comes to the family or their own collections. A percentage of them will likely move on to become connoisseurs. Hence, let's now consider how ultra-wealthy connoisseurs make certain key collecting decisions.

DECISION-MAKING INFLUENCES

When it comes to the ultra-wealthy, there are very powerful delineations among Cubs, Collectors, and Connoisseurs. A place where this is particularly apparent and noteworthy is how they often make acquisition decisions. The extent to which different influencers play a role is usually very pronounced (Exhibit 12.6).

EXHIBIT 12.6 Decision-Making Influences

INFLUENCES	CUBS	COLLECTORS	CONNOISSEURS
Media	Medium to High	Medium	Very Low to Non-Existent
Referential group	Medium	Medium	Low
Intermediaries	Very High	High	Cooperative
Personal research	Low	Low to High	Very High

Media consists of the messages centered on the field of interest such as advertising and public relations. They're usually uni-directional; they do not require a response. Magazines, for instance, can be used to derive insights on specific items in a field of interest. With respect to acquiring luxury products and services, media plays an important and sometimes determining role. When it comes to collecting, media is influential with Cubs, and when perceived as authoritative can influence Collectors as well. These two groups make up over 90% of Collectors.

Because of their lack of expertise, Cubs turn to media for ideas as well as a way to learn about specific items. Cubs also gain initial interest in categories from media. Initial casual purchases combined with media can lead to more serious interest in the category. Collectors, meanwhile, are many times less inclined to use media in this manner as they've come to rely more on themselves, intermediaries, and specialty guides or acknowledged experts. Highly regarded authorities in media can be valuable in reaching this group. In other words, Collectors consume media but with a high level of scrutiny. For Connoisseurs, the media has minimal if any impact as they've personally developed the requisite expertise. In fact, Connoisseurs see their viewpoints as better informed than what is generally available through media.

Referential group refers to peers or other people the ultra-wealthy look to as role models. An undisputed leading authority in a field of interest would be somewhat impactful on all three segments, but less so with respect to Connoisseurs as they've likely developed their own strong, well-reasoned opinions.

Intermediaries are professionals directly involved in helping the ultra-wealthy acquire and prune substantial collections. Their knowledge, experience, and skills are often of extreme importance to Cubs and Collectors. The selection of these professionals should be approached like all other experts employed by the ultra-wealthy (see *Chapter 9: Selecting Professional Advisors*).

Connoisseurs, on the other hand, work with intermediaries very differently than Cubs or Collectors. Because of the extensive understandings Connoisseurs bring to the table, they tend to deal with intermediaries as colleagues.

Personal research refers to the actions taken by the ultra-wealthy by their own efforts to become expert and remain so concerning their field of interest. This occurs through dedication, education, and experience.

Cubs, as they're new to serious collecting, generally lack the competencies to rely on themselves without professional assistance. The importance of personal research for Collectors ranges the gamut from those who will not feel expert enough to make unaided decision to those who readily do. For Collectors, the value of their own research is usually quite situational.

Connoisseurs, in contrast, rely heavily on their own learned opinions. While they'll often incorporate the perspectives of others, collecting is more than a hobby or even a passion; it's (as noted above) an area of mastery and a source of well-being. Critically, collecting is central to their identities (see above).

A percentage of ultra-wealthy inheritors are going to take a meaningful decision-making position with respect to collecting. Moreover, a percentage of these exceptionally affluent individuals will become Connoisseurs. Let's look at the data indicating where and how the ultra-wealthy inheritors will be involved.

TAKING THE REINS

We find that within those exceptionally affluent families with major collections, about half of the ultra-wealthy inheritors with personal or family collections are looking to become more significantly involved in managing them (Exhibit 12.7). This is especially the case among the individual ultra-wealthy inheritors.

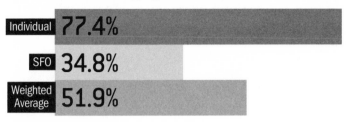

EXHIBIT 12.7 Will Become Significantly More Involved in Managing the Collections

N = 77 ultra-wealthy inheritors

In a related vein, more than half of all ultra-wealthy inheritors are personally motivated to create or expand a substantial collection (Exhibit 12.8). Again, a larger percentage of the individual ultra-wealthy inheritors feel this way. Still overall, when it comes to the process of collecting, we see ultra-wealthy inheritors very clearly taking the reins.

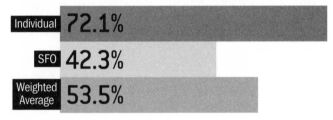

EXHIBIT 12.8 Will Become Significantly More Involved in Creating or Expanding a Collection

N = 114 ultra-wealthy inheritors

What's clear is that for most ultra-wealthy inheritors whose families do collect, or who are collectors in their own right, the use of intermediaries is usually essential. These specialists are needed in procuring pieces for the collection as well as culling it.

As there are often tax considerations to address, professional advisors are habitually needed. Presently, about 45% of the ultra-wealthy inheritors are focused on the tax issues with less than 10% of individual ultra-wealthy inheritors compared to 70% of SFO ultra-wealthy inheritors focused on the matter (Exhibit 12.9).

EXHIBIT 12.9 Tax Management and Protection

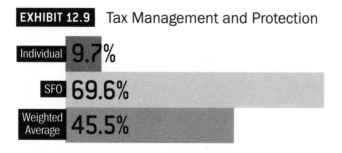

N = 77 ultra-wealthy inheritors

CONCLUSION

We've briefly examined ultra-wealthy Connoisseurs—a small but highly prominent seg-ments of the exceptionally affluent who are amassing substantial collections. This elite segment not only strongly impacts their fields of interest, but the ripple effect of their actions also affects the broader collector culture as well as aspects of high-end luxury products and services.

What Connoisseurs are not are passion investors, nor are they compulsive. Instead, Connoisseurs are amazingly erudite and remarkable students when it comes to their fields of interest—their collections. While they employ intermediaries, as needed, to assist them in addressing their collections, these relationships with these authorities are usually very cooperative.

Concurrently, many ultra-wealthy inheritors are likely to be involved in their own or their family's collections. What's quite telling is that, we expect, a keen number of ultra-wealthy inheritors are very likely to become highly involved with creating ever-greater substantial collections. A solid percentage of them will likely become Connoisseurs. As such, we anticipate—as they'll accomplish with their philanthropic agendas (see *Chapter 5: Philanthropy*)—they'll act as transformative agents in their fields of interest.

Douglas D. Gollan is a recognized authority on the ultra-high-net-worth lifestyle. He co-founded Elite Traveler Media Group in 2001, publisher of the award-winning Elite Traveler *magazine (www.elitetraveler.com), distributed worldwide aboard private jets. He is co-author of* The Sky's the Limit, *a book studying buying motivators of ultra-high-net-worth consumers.*

CHAPTER

13

BARGAINING BRILLIANCE

by Russ Alan Prince & Frank Carone

AN AREA WHERE ULTRA-WEALTHY inheritors are interested in enhancing their knowledge and skills is in negotiations (see *Chapter 4: Enhancing Expertise*). It isn't that they're not capable negotiators, but many of them recognize they can ratchet up their abilities. Even small, incremental improvements translate multiplicatively into superior outcomes. Furthermore, a heightened level of expertise at negotiating and networking has multifarious applications where ultra-wealthy inheritors are taking the reins.

By being better bargainers, ultra-wealthy inheritors can be more effective with charitable and supportive organizations. At the same time, they can be more adept at helping eleemosynary institutions raise funds. When it comes to deal making, negotiating prowess is of critical importance whether on the sales or buy side of the table. As ultra-wealthy inheritors are becoming ever more involved in selecting professional advisors (see *Chapter 9: Selecting Professional Advisors*), by being more proficient negotiators, they're more likely to be able to get partisan and superior arrangements.

As noted, while many ultra-wealthy inheritors are quite capable, they recognize the advantages they can gain by improving slightly. In researching and consulting with extreme wealth creators, we've been able to develop a highly systemic approach to negotiation we refer to as bargaining brilliance. While this approach is exceptionally effective due to its foundational elements, we recognize it doesn't philosophically appeal to everyone.

Let's begin with the foundation of the methodology.

"I WIN, YOU WHATEVER"

The "I win, you whatever" philosophy doesn't mean that one party in a negotiation must be a winner and the other party must be a loser. Both parties can certainly conclude the negotiations as winners, which is the optimal scenario. However, the "I win, you whatever" philosophy says that it's essential for success to walk away a winner, irrespective of the ability of the other party to reach his or her goals.

Simply put, wealth creators realize that the only way they're going to win when negotiating is by carefully and forcefully looking out for their own interests. This is not about being selfish or egotistical, it's about being realistic. It's the way to succeed.

While advocates of the win-win philosophy frequently talk about long-term relationships and fairness for all, according to most self-made wealth creators, if you're not looking out for yourself, it's highly unlikely anyone you're negotiating with will be looking out for you. To see the potential alternatives, consider the matrix in Exhibit 13.1.

EXHIBIT 13.1 Negotiating Results Matrix

		YOU	
		Lose	Win
ADVERSARY	**Win**	Substandard	Optimal
	Lose	Substandard	Excellent

Source: I Win, You Whatever (2013)

The optimal scenario is one where all parties conclude the negotiations as winners. If everyone cannot be successful, as long as you yourself achieve your goals, then the negotiations are still a success. If you lose, whether your adversary wins or loses, for you the result of the negotiation was substandard.

This philosophy is at the core of the way many wealth creators bargain, and it's part of the reason they're repeatedly so effective. While they usually have no problem with seeing their adversaries doing well, they themselves *must win*.

THE PERFORMANCE EQUATION

Extreme wealth creators usually approach negotiating business deals, for instance, in what are often profoundly different ways than less financially successful individuals. Whether establishing joint ventures, creating strategic alliances, or selling and buying companies, not only are they exceedingly focused and disciplined, but they also employ an array of strategies and tactics likely to radically increase their ability to achieve the outcomes they're looking for. They're effective at getting the terms they want and structuring the deal for their benefit.

Through in depth research of these wealth creators, we identified the various components of highly successful negotiating, and at its core is the performance equation:

$$\text{Perspective} + \text{Purpose} + \text{Preparation} + \text{Process} = \textbf{PERFORMANCE}$$

Let's briefly examine each of the variables in this performance equation.

Perspective is a person's bargaining mind-set. It's his or her mental orientation to be highly successful when negotiating. The negotiator intensely focuses on achieving his or her agenda, maintaining a single mindedness toward goals to which all else outside of this is noise. It's paramount to be aware that a person's mind-set is foundational to negotiating success.

SELECT KEY CONCEPTS

- **Everyone—yes, everyone—is dysfunctional.** The negotiator's intent is to gain an advantage by understanding, and thereby own, the other parties issues, while avoiding letting the people sitting on the other side of the table to exploit his or her dysfunctional characteristics.

- **Success breeds "enemies."** This is a structural phenomenon resulting in some of the best negotiators often being vilified. As such, antagonistic feelings from the less prosperous side are inevitable, and it's important for a negotiator not to let the possibility of becoming denigrated be an impediment to achieving significant results.

Purpose is what a negotiator wants out of the negotiation. It's the outcomes he or she is looking for. Extreme wealth creators are very good at defining their range of goals and maintaining their focus on the high-end of these ranges because they conscientiously and thoroughly establish them in advance of commencing a negotiation. Moreover, they're proficient at connecting their negotiating goals to their overall business goals and related objectives.

SELECT KEY CONCEPTS

- **The negotiating goals need to be slightly unreasonable.** Negotiating goals are very likely to prove motivating and attainable when they make enough sense to the opponent, but still make that person effectively uneasy. This requires an intense understanding of the rationale—on all sides—for the goals.

- **Sticking to high-end goals is regularly essential.** Many negotiators in trying to make a deal make bad ones as they surrender on critical terms. This not only results in remorse, but it can also contribute to subsequent actions that derail future opportunities. Astute negotiators understand that no deal is infinitely better than a bad deal and define their limits in advance of a negotiation.

Preparation is the work the negotiator conducts before the facing off with his or her adversary. It's how a person evaluates the character of the negotiation, the overall strategic approach he or she chooses to take, the formulation of key arguments, and how he or she derives—or intends to derive—advantages. To obtain the best results, negotiators prepare intensely, if not passionately: they have a plan.

SELECT KEY CONCEPTS

- **Negotiate the people.** While understanding the terms of a deal, for instance, is very important, success will more likely come from understanding the people sitting across the table. Being attuned to their dysfunction (see above), their need for the deal, their alternatives and other relevant issues and concerns, can greatly empower a negotiator.

- **Candidly evaluate the situation.** An honest assessment of the relative position a negotiator has vis-a-vie his or her adversary will dictate the most appropriate bargaining strategies to employ. Depending on the respective advantages each side has, the need to be clever can become integral.

Process is the give and take between parties in the negotiation. It's how a person makes his or her case based on the previous stage tempered by the way the interaction is progressing. What's habitually central to being effective at this time is the nature and quality of the relationship between the negotiating parties.

SELECT KEY CONCEPTS

- **Active listening is a cornerstone skill.** High-caliber negotiators truly capture and understand the messages other people are sending. It includes assessing nonverbal as well as verbal messages. Active listening also entails understanding the context—the current situation, the person, and scenario's back story as well as the person's expectations.

- **A negotiator who can make anger work for him or her has a distinct advantage over an opponent.** By not letting anger get in the way, a negotiator can avoid magnifying insecurities, which can produce more anger, cloud reason, and result in poor decision making. Meanwhile, fostering anger in adversaries can prove quite beneficial.

IMPLICATION

Bargaining brilliance with the "I win, you whatever" philosophy at its core embodies the best negotiating thinking and practices of extreme wealth creators. Many ultra-wealthy inheritors have expressed a desire to become more efficacious when it comes to bargaining. From increasing the effectiveness of their philanthropic endeavors to being more effectual when doing deals to being able to craft superior arrangements when employing professionals, the ability of ultra-wealthy inheritors to bargain brilliantly can make a resounding difference.

What's evident in working with the ultra-wealthy is that many of them are quite capable negotiators, yet are interested in stepping-up their expertise. At the same time, bargaining brilliance is very learnable. There aren't any secrets to negotiating at this level of proficiency, as the knowledge—the know-how—is easily accessible. Negotiating success, therefore, is much more a matter of doing than know-how.

Frank V. Carone is a Partner at Abrams, Fensterman, Fensterman, Eisman, Formato, Ferrara & Wolf, LLP (www.abramslaw.com). Frank has extensive experience in many complex areas of the law including Criminal Defense, Regulatory Compliance, Banking, Litigation and Corporate Governance. Attorneys and members of the profession on mortgage compliance, litigation, corporate governance, and complex criminal matters consult him regularly.

CHAPTER
14

STREET-SMART
NETWORKING

by Russ Alan Prince & Brett Van Bortel

ULTRA-WEALTHY INHERITORS due to their family and personal relationships usually have very extensive and significant networks (see *Chapter 4: Enhancing Expertise*). Without question, a percentage of ultra-wealthy inheritors are quite adept at leveraging many of these contacts. However, in numerous situations they're not being as effective as they possibly could. Even among these more adept networkers, there's often a strong desire to become ever more proficient.

Capable networking regularly is a critical skill set to all manner of personal and professional success. It dovetails with the noted interests of ultra-wealthy inheritors such as philanthropy (see *Chapter 5: Philanthropy*). Thus, they're increasingly able to connect with like-minded individuals and institutions to share insights and best practices as well as to possibly work jointly. Another keen interest of ultra-wealthy inheritors is deal-making (see *Chapter 7: Doing Deals*). Critical to this is the ability to source deals that is vastly facilitated by skilled networking. Additionally, with the high interest in club deals, the capacity to strategically network among their peers is essential.

In working with the ultra-wealthy to raise capital for new business ventures as well as for alternative investment funds they manage (see below), we consistently find that they're easily able to bring in hundreds of millions of dollars by going out no further than three levels. The key is to identify potential investors based on their needs and wants as well as their concerns and obstacles (see below).

All in all, a meaningful number of ultra-wealthy inheritors are very interested in becoming more proficient networkers. In consulting with and developing educational programs (see *Chapter 11: The Education of Global Stewards*) for the exceptionally affluent in this and other areas, it's clear they have distinct and powerful advantages due to a variety of factors such as their fortunes and their formal as well as informal edification (see *Chapter 2: Inheriting More Than Money*). Their motivation and commitment also prove instrumental.

STREET-SMART NETWORKING

Without question, ultra-wealthy inheritors are primarily and extensively connected to others in four interrelated ways—personal, family, social, and business. Sometimes, the breadth and depth of their networks work against them generating too many possibilities. This in turn results in stagnation because of decision paralysis and fear of regret. The conundrum for ultra-wealthy inheritors is how to unlock and leverage their often-amazing database of contacts to foster their philanthropic, professional, and personal goals.

We've dissected the networking philosophies and strategies of extreme wealth creators. We've distilled the best practices of these hyper-successful individuals. While derived using academic rigor, we refer to this approach as "street-smart networking" because it's predicated on an astute ability to read people, recognize angles, and integrate all of this to achieve set goals.

Critical to the networking effectiveness of extreme wealth creators is their ability to create advocates. These are individuals possessing highly beneficial resources and connections who are firmly and ardently on the side of the extreme wealth creators. The advocates are regularly few in number, but they're instrumental in enabling the wealth creator to create significant fortunes as well as achieve other goals such as charitable ones.

Some or all of the advocates may work on a particular endeavor or across a series of undertakings. It's not that there aren't other people—potentially lots and lots of other people—with whom a person will work to make things happen. It's just that advocates are the critical participants in the wealth creator's network.

THE STREET-SMART NETWORKING EQUATION

In determining the negotiating best practices of significant wealth creators, we've been able to codify the way their highly effective network operates. We summarized this methodology in the following street-smart networking equation:

Aspirations + Agenda + Assessments + Alignment = **ADVOCATES > ACHIEVEMENTS**

Aspirations. Street-smart networking starts with aspirations. A person's aspirations can readily change as circumstances change. Moreover, while the larger goals such as becoming substantially wealthier or helping find a cure for breast cancer tend to remain consistent, the interim objectives are usually prone to revisions in order to be responsive to changing situational considerations. Extreme wealth creators regularly set high but grounded aspirations. They're looking to succeed in a big way and, at the same time, they're wise enough not to make these goals just fantasies.

Agenda. With goals in place, wealth creators will think through what they have to do and prepare. In effect, they put together a plan. It's certainly not enough to "want." A pronounced differentiator between those who excel and the rest of the population is the effort to think through and act. This solidly begins with the agenda.

Assessments. Unequivocally, central to creating and maintaining a cohesive network of advocates are assessments. They're at the very core of extraordinary networking success. This is where the street-smart networker develops a deep understanding of the people he or she is dealing with. Because of the pivotal role assessments play in street-smart networking, it's discussed in greater detail below.

Alignment. With extreme wealth creators, knowing what they're striving to accomplish and having identified the people who can prove helpful, there's then the need for alignment. There needs to be a "set of mutual motivations" that ties the parties together.

Effectively aligning interests is squarely predicated on street-smarts. It's often an exercise in ingenuity and shrewdness. Aligning interests is usually based on a deep understanding of people's critical concerns first, and his or her expressed intent secondarily. These issues are then balanced by the other components of the assessment (see below). This usually results in a multi-layered array of provocations and incentives, which can be truly binding and driving.

Achievements. The results from working with advocates are constantly evaluated against aspirations. In effect, the achievements are consistently being critiqued. These critical appraisals enable wealth creators to perpetually refine and enhance their network. This might entail anything from tweaking the mechanisms of alignment to changing the people with whom they're working.

Because of the central role played by assessments, let's look at the Assessment Instrument.

THE ASSESSMENT INSTRUMENT

Assessments are central to creating and maintaining a cohesive team of advocates. It's a foundational element to extraordinary networking success. By intensely and proactively determining the ways a potential advocate can contribute as well as be appropriately motivated, extreme wealth creators are able to get the range and level of support desired.

EXHIBIT 14.1   Assessment Instrument

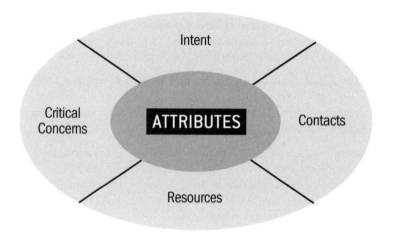

Source: Street-Smart Networking (2014)

The following are the broad-brush components of the information sought in the Assessment Instrument (Exhibit 14.1):

- **Attributes** are the central and often defining characteristics of the person. Aside from demographics, included here are his or her strengths and weaknesses. Special attention should be paid to the individual's expertise and particular competencies.

- **Contacts** are the people the individual knows and can access. As noted above, these relationships are usually a function of business, social, family, and personal associations. It's very important to understand not only the number of relationships, but also the quality of the relationship the person has with these other people. Very often a person acting as a "connector once or twice removed" can also be extremely powerful, which necessitates learning about the person's extended contacts.

- **Resources** are the "assets" and means at the person's disposal. They can be under his or her direct or indirect influence or control, or available as a function of close relationships. The objective is to first identify these resources and then to discern how they can be adeptly leveraged. It's not uncommon for many resources to not be "appreciated" by the individual, but that doesn't in any way diminish their value.

- **Intent** refers to the individual's preferences, needs, and wants as they translate into interim objectives, which feed into larger goals. Included here is what he or she is seeking to attain financially, professionally, and personally. It's useful to identify the gap between where the person is today and where he or she wants to be as well as the principal obstacles in the way. The most precarious obstacles might or might not be recognized by the individual.

- **Crucial concerns** are the dominant and persuasive issues and interests the person is presently dealing with. These matters prove to be of overriding importance as they're habitually forefront in the person's mind. They're the high-priority matters that will dramatically impact the person's entire decision-making as well as his or her ability to focus and implement. Of tremendous importance are the areas of dysfunction and accomplishment as they regularly have a pronounced impact on behavior.

As noted, ultra-wealthy inheritors are often exceedingly well connected. What's also periodically the case is that they're not leveraging their relationships as effectively as they can (see *Chapter 4: Enhancing Expertise*). The following case study describes an ultra-wealthy inheritor consulting client who used the street-smart networking framework to raise a little more than US$500 million for a new hedge fund.

RAISING CAPITAL: CASE STUDY

The scion—third generation—of an exceptionally affluent family working in their family office wanted to launch a new hedge fund where he would put together the investment team and manage the monies. His family seeded the fund to the tune of approximately US$40 million. He was responsible to raise additional funds and was restricted from going to existing relationships of the family or their single-family office. His intent was to have a hedge fund totaling US$200 million, which meant he had to raise an additional US$160 million from investors he personally sourced.

After about six months of knocking on doors of institutional investors, third-party marketers, and people he knew, he hadn't brought any money to his hedge fund. This lack of success led to adopting a capital raising approach based on a bespoke street-smart networking methodology. The following is a very simplified outline of the approach (Exhibit 14.2):

Step 1: Preparations. Before approaching anyone, three preparatory business development actions were taken.

1. His very extensive list of contacts was evaluated and high-potential individuals were identified.

2. A customized assessment instrument was developed.

3. A "template narrative" was constructed.

Step 2: Evaluations. Using the customized assessment instrument, likely investors were assessed from his high-potential list.

Step 3: Solicitations. The evaluations coupled with the template narrative resulted in highly individualized narratives for each "probable" investor.

EXHIBIT 14.2   Bespoke Street-Smart Networking Methodology

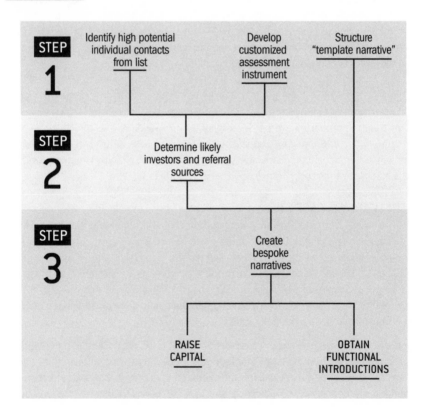

This approach resulted in monies provided to the hedge fund as well as functional intro-ductions to other potential investors. The hedge fund was closed having raised slightly more than US$500 million (including the seed capital)—an amount way beyond what was originally thought possible.

What's critical to understand is that the success of this capital raise was predominantly a function of the ultra-wealthy inheritor's very extensive and powerful network. The street-smart networking framework was just the way to capitalize on these outstanding relationships.

IMPLICATION

Without a doubt, a preponderance of ultra-wealthy inheritors have truly amazing personal and professional contacts due strongly to their own efforts augmented at times by the relationships of their families. However, relatively few of them are doing as much as they conceivably can to effectively leverage, let alone maximize, the diverse and consequen-tial value of these relationships.

Street-smart networking is an inordinately formidable framework that ultra-wealthy inher-itors can employ to capitalize on their broad and deep array of existing relationships as well as extend their network in the service of dramatic results. It's a way of exponentially multiplying the value of their relationships to achieve extraordinary goals.

OWNING THE TRUST: HOW TO MAINTAIN CONTROL AND FLEXIBILITY

by Edward W. Renn

MANY SUCCESSFUL FAMILIES have used trusts to minimize taxes as they pass significant assets to the next generation. Properly drafted, trusts can also protect assets from the claims of tort or contract creditors and divorcing spouses.

Trusts accomplish many positive things that outright, individual ownership cannot. Minimizing taxes and protecting assets from unjust claims are objectives nearly everyone can agree on. Whether you are now drafting trusts to benefit your family or hold an inheritance in a trust drafted decades ago, you can achieve control and flexibility for you and your family members while reducing taxes and protecting assets.

In many traditional trusts, achieving these objectives requires the family to give up control and hope the trustee serves them well. Why rely on a hope and a prayer when there are ways to better insure that the family's goals are attained? Trust law has evolved rapidly, creating new options that allow for greater family control, which simply did not exist or were not commonly used when many current trusts were established.

Many trusts set up decades ago appoint a corporate entity, usually a bank or trust company, as the trustee. These professional fiduciaries provide certain advantages. They have experience serving as trustee, are well versed in fiduciary duties, and they maintain detailed records. It takes more than organizational skills to be the right trustee for a trust. Does the institutional trustee know how to get the most out of the assets held in trust? Especially when the trust's assets consist of a family business, a family member involved in the business would likely be in a better position to direct how these assets are managed.

While corporate trustees have a fiduciary duty to serve you and your family, at the end of the day they also have a duty to produce a profit for their shareholders. These corporate trustees charge fees and have a real financial interest in retaining control over the trust. They also try to avoid controversy, and if a dispute among beneficiaries breaks out, they often become passive and look to a court to instruct them. You can't rely on an independent entity to think and act solely in your best interest. You need to take ownership.

POWER TO REMOVE A TRUSTEE

Who is serving as your trustee will have a large impact on how trust assets perform and how they are distributed. It is crucial to serve as a check and balance to a trustee. A simple yet effective power that gives you and your family the ability to ensure you have the right trustee in place is the power to remove and replace the trustee. The power to remove a trustee incentivizes the trustee to manage the assets well and make distributions when appropriate. No matter what other interests the trustee may have or what their preferences may be for managing the trust, if the trustee wants to remain as trustee and you have the power to remove, the trustee needs to listen.

At a minimum, a dialogue should take place in which the trustee explains the economic or legal reasons why they are reluctant to make an investment or distribution. Many older trusts without a trustee removal provision leave beneficiaries in a position where they need to go to court to have a trustee removed for cause. This is both expensive and time consuming. A simple provision providing that you have the power to remove a trustee for any reason gives you efficient control over your trust.

When you remove a sole trustee, you need to appoint a new one, as a trust must always have a trustee. There are certain limitations on who you can appoint, or you endanger the trust's tax and creditor protection benefits. You can't appoint yourself as trustee with distribution power over an "absolute discretion" trust if you are a beneficiary, but who can you appoint?

The answer is almost anyone except yourself, your spouse, your children, other close family members, or your employees. That means, your trusted family advisor, your best friend from college, another bank with which you have a close relationship, your accountant, your lawyer, and pretty much anyone else can serve as your trustee. This ability to remove a trustee coupled with the ability to appoint almost anyone as trustee is an effective mechanism to keep control over the person with the ability to make distributions, but what about being part of the decision making process?

BE A TRUSTEE

To get the tax minimization and creditor protection from a trust, the beneficiaries cannot have the power to make distributions. However, making distributions is just one function of the trustee. In preserving and growing a family's wealth, how the assets are managed is just as important as making distributions. You, your spouse, and children can serve alongside another "independent" trustee or trustees and have all powers of a trustee *except for* the power to make distributions.

Combining the ability to serve as a "family" or "non-independent" trustee with the ability to remove the "independent" trustee who has distribution powers, gives you control and flexibility over the management and performance of your trust. For example, you could have your closest friend (so long as he is not closely related or employed by you or a company you control) serve as your co-trustee with distribution powers. You can be comfortable that he will make distributions to you and your family when they are appropriate. However, if your friend's performance as trustee is not good, you can remove and replace him with someone who would be better suited to the position.

Additionally, this independent person can delegate to a beneficiary, as co-trustee, some of his or her investment and management powers, which effectively allows the beneficiary to directly control and manage the assets of the trust. Despite the significant control this provides, the beneficiary should still receive all of the tax and creditor protection trusts have to offer.

DIRECT YOUR TRUSTEE

Ancient and arcane trust provisions often appoint institutional trustees who give you little control over the trust while imposing significant fees and expenses. Because trust law has evolved, it is now possible to get the benefits of an institutional trustee while retaining control and minimizing the financial costs. There are two significant benefits that an institutional trustee can provide that cannot be obtained with individual trustees (i.e. the college roommate).

First, institutional trustees have a great deal of experience and capability in managing trusts and keeping detailed and accurate records of a trust's property and transactions. This makes the preparation of tax returns and accountings easier. It also institutionalizes knowledge in a way that is simply not possible with an individual trustee.

The second primary benefit to an institutional trustee is that the trust can be located in a state of your choosing. Just like a corporation, a partnership, or any other legal entity, a trust must be formed under the laws of a single state. While it is possible to establish a trust in any of the 50 states, some states are better than others.

There is no perfect jurisdiction for every type of trust or every family situation. In some situations, privacy may be key, while in others protecting trust property from potential divorces or minimizing state taxes may be the driving force. Allowing trusts to exist for an unlimited period of time, protecting assets from creditors, sophisticated and beneficiary friendly courts, and modern statutory provisions for trusts, are all a factor of state law. If you or your trusted individual trustee does not live in the jurisdiction that optimizes your trust, you will need an institutional presence to achieve your goals.

Delaware, South Dakota, Nevada, New Hampshire, Alaska, and Wyoming are some of the states with modern trust provisions that have attracted non-residents to establish trusts. Each state has its own specific advantages, and a local institutional trustee gives the trust access to the state law of choice.

Having an institutional trustee in a state with modern trust provisions allows you and your trust to escape the restraints and minimize the fees traditionally associated with institutional trustees. Certain states, such as Delaware, South Dakota, Nevada, and New Hampshire allow for "directed trustees."

What differentiates a directed trustee from a traditional trustee is right in the name—they are "directed." Directed trustees do not make distribution or investment decisions; they are directed to take such actions by appointed advisors. To get the most control over a trust, you can bifurcate the decisions a trustee can make into categories—distributions, investments, and administration.

A distribution advisor should be an independent person (i.e. unrelated and not employed by the grantor or beneficiary in some way) who directs the directed trustee to make distributions. An investment advisor, who could be you as the grantor or beneficiary, directs the directed trustee on what investments to make. With states that allow for directed trustees, the directed trustee must follow the instructions of the advisor. The directed trustee does not have the independent decision-making authority and responsibility of a traditional trustee. Therefore, because liability is significant lower, directed trustees' fees should be lower than those charged by traditional institutional trustees.

Having a directed trustee can provide great benefits at a modest cost. By having a directed trustee, you can establish a trust or move an existing trust to a jurisdiction that provides additional benefits to you, your family, and your trust. You, or another person, could have the power to remove the directed trustee at some future point if the arrangement is no longer beneficial.

You do not have to worry about the directed trustee going "maverick" and not following instructions from the advisors. You could have "trustee like" power to manage trust assets by serving as the investment advisor. You can have a friend serve as distribution advisor, and you could retain the power to remove the distribution advisor. You get your choice of jurisdiction and the professional trust administration, record keeping, tax preparation, and reporting provided by an institutional trustee.

OWN YOUR TRUSTEE

Another alternative to having a traditional institutional trustee is to create your own corporate trustee, commonly referred to as a "private trust company," that you and other family members own. Private trust companies have existed for quite sometime. Some of the largest public trust companies in existence today began as private trust companies.

Private trust companies are not trusts themselves. Instead, it is a family essentially creating its own institutional trustee. Instead of hiring a bank or trust company, which are owned by others, you could use your private trust company to act as trustee of your trusts.

By owning the private trust company, your family can collectively pick its own members and trusted independent individuals to serve on the trust company's board of directors. The private trust company itself will divide the duties of a trustee among various committees, including a committee to manage distributions, a committee to manage trust assets, and a committee to amend the rules of the trust company. Committees ensure the trusts served by the private trust company retain tax and creditor protected status by having independent members of the board make distribution decisions.

There are costs associated with creating, running and staffing a private trust company, but having this custom structure is a perfect fit for certain very wealthy families. For a family with many trusts established over the years with different trustees, consolidating all of the trusts under a single trustee owned by the family could provide cost reduction and a level of coordination and continuity among the trusts that would not otherwise be possible. This could prove especially useful when multiple trusts hold interests in a single asset, such as the family business. Significant cost savings as compared to traditional trust companies are likely if the family's wealth held in trusts is significant.

HOW TO GET THE TRUST YOU WANT

If you are creating a new trust, it is easy to get a tax optimal, creditor protected, administratively flexible vehicle by selecting the right lawyer and correct jurisdiction. If you are the beneficiary of an existing trust that does not maximize tax savings or creditor protection or does not provide sufficiently flexible trust administration, it may still be possible to achieve some or all of these benefits by modifying certain provisions (see below).

In addition, an existing sub-optimal trust could be used to leverage the assets in a new trust to increase its growth potential. This can be accomplished by the existing trust loaning funds to the new trust with a long-term promissory note with annual interest-only payments and a balloon payment at maturity. Interest rates on related party loans up to nine years have been below 2% for the last several years. If the new trust is able to earn a return that is better than 2%, all of the additional growth will remain in the new trust. This technique effectively freezes the existing trust to grow assets in the new trust. Preferred Partnerships can also achieve this freeze.

CHANGING YOUR EXISTING TRUST

Your existing trust may have been created at a time when administrative flexibility was not available. Perhaps personal, family, or economic circumstances have changed in a manner that was not anticipated by the grantor. The trust assets may be substantially larger than expected at the outset, or a change in federal or state tax law may now warrant a change to minimize the tax bite.

Creditor protection may be a bigger issue now than it was at inception, perhaps because of the risk of divorce or a beneficiary entering a profession that is a target for unwarranted litigation (e.g. entrepreneur, doctor, lawyer, real estate developer, etc.). Further, modern trust laws offer substantial flexibility and benefits that simply were not available when the trust was first created. The following mechanisms can be utilized, where possible, to achieve the desired benefits.

Amendment. An irrevocable trust agreement may include a provision permitting the trustee to alter the administrative provisions of the trust by amendment. Often, an amendment can be implemented with relative ease by a willing and cooperative trustee by simply signing the desired amendment.

Administrative amendments can typically be used to change trustee provisions, for example, to create a directed trust structure (if permitted by law) or add a beneficiary as a co-trustee to participate in the investment and management of the trust property. However, because administrative amendments relate only to administrative provisions, they cannot be used to change distribution provisions or extend the term of a trust.

Trust Decanting. "Decanting" refers to a trustee exercising his distribution power by making a distribution of trust property into a new trust for the benefit of the old trust's beneficiaries. It is similar to decanting red wine; the fluid is poured out of the bottle (the old trust) and into the decanter (the new trust). The new trust can include many updated trust provisions, but decanting is a technique that is not available in every situation and will depend on the provisions of trust agreement and the governing law of the trust.

As a preliminary matter, decanting is limited by the extent of the trustee's authority to make a distribution in trust. The trustee must have the ability to make a distribution of principal for the benefit of the beneficiaries. If the trustee's discretion to make distributions is "absolute", the trustee can generally decant. If the trustee's discretion is more restrictive, for example, if the trustee can only make "ascertainable" distributions for a beneficiary's health, education, maintenance or support, the trustee generally cannot decant unless there is an applicable state decanting statute.

Decanting can typically be accomplished without court approval unless the trust is subject to court supervision (e.g. a testamentary trust created in a person's Will). However, it may be necessary to change the governing law of the trust in order to be able to use another state's more favorable laws, which may necessitate changing the trustee.

Court Modification. If amendment or decanting are not available, the trustee (and in some cases, the beneficiaries) can petition a court to modify an existing trust agreement.

This can be a more arduous and costly process because of the involvement of a court, and the ultimate outcome is less certain.

A court judgment provides assurance that the modification is valid, which can be particularly important if a disgruntled beneficiary or creditor is likely to challenge the modification in an attempt to access trust property that was potentially available under the old trust provisions. As an example, assume a trust was to terminate when a beneficiary reached age 40 and, at age 39, the beneficiary was in the middle of a divorce. In such a case, if the trustee modified the trust term to continue the trust for the beneficiary's lifetime, the divorcing spouse has an incentive to challenge this modification because a complete distribution of trust property at age 40 could have a favorable impact on the divorce settlement. A court modification is typically more difficult to challenge than an amendment or trust decanting done as an exercise of the trustee's powers.

Exercise of a Power of Appointment. As a beneficiary, you may have been granted a "power of appointment" exercisable during your life or at death. A "limited power of appointment" allows you to appoint trust property among a group of permitted appointees not including yourself (but typically including your descendants). If you have such a power, you can direct the trust property into a trust with updated provisions. You can use this power to subdivide your existing trust or transfer a trust to younger family members who need the assets but would be better served by a different trust structure.

While this option is completely within your control, the drawback is that you would not be able to benefit from the new trust. This is why only part of a trust's assets is frequently appointed to a new trust. In some cases, this power may best be exercised at your death, which would typically be accomplished in your Will. The benefit to this power is that you have greater flexibility to craft the new trust provisions than a trustee would have in an amendment or a trust decanting or a court would have in a modification.

You may also have been granted a "general power of appointment" in a trust. This type of power allows you to appoint trust property to a group of permitted appointees including yourself. However, if you have such a power, the trust property remaining at your death will be included in your taxable estate for estate tax purposes regardless of whether you exercise the power. As a result, a general power of appointment should be factored in to your personal planning. With a general power, you have unlimited flexibility.

Limitations. There are several limitations to the changes that can be made through an amendment, trust decanting, court modification, and even the exercise of a limited power of appointment. Specifically, none of the foregoing mechanisms can be used to extend the term of the trust for a period longer than the maximum duration under the law at the time that the trust was created.

If a beneficiary has a current mandatory right to receive income annually, that right cannot be taken away. Further, if the existing trust is not subject to generation-skipping transfer tax, it is important that a decant, court modification, or exercise of a limited power of appointment be structured properly to ensure that the generation-skipping transfer tax exempt status of the trust property is not lost.

There are pitfalls to careless trust modification, including loss of important tax benefits, but the potential advantages are great and can often be achieved with careful planning.

CONCLUSION

You should not be passive when it comes to your role as a trust grantor or beneficiary. Having an inheritance in trust can provide creditor protection that you cannot easily obtain, in addition to significant potential tax savings. And, you can have control with respect to the investment and management of the trust property. By taking a proactive approach, you are not only a beneficiary—you are effectively an owner.

Edward A. Renn is a principal in the international law firm, Withers Bergman LLP (www.withersworldwide.com). Ed focuses on domestic and international private client matters. He provides legal advice to families, trustees, and beneficiaries on U.S. and international estate and income tax planning, wealth preservation, trust structuring and administration, and business succession planning. Ed is a frequent speaker and writer, and has co-authored several books on estate planning.

SOPHISTICATED ADVANCED PLANNING USING LIFE INSURANCE

by Frank W. Seneco & Evan Jehle

A GOOD WAY TO THINK about life insurance for the very wealthy is that it's like a Swiss Army knife—highly versatile and very useful. As a stand-alone solution or as part of advanced tax planning, life insurance can be an exceedingly powerful tool.

In working with the ultra-wealthy, the possibilities provided by the astute use of life insurance multiply due to the assets involved—amount and structure—and their regularly complex personal and professional lives. In providing life insurance based solutions to the ultra-wealthy, we find their needs range from creating a straight-forward optimal life insurance portfolio to intricate business funding mechanisms to addressing complicated personal and family conditions.

Recognizing there are many possibilities when it comes to the ultra-wealthy to employ life insurance based solutions, we'll briefly consider three scenarios:

- Foreign nationals benefiting from U.S. life insurance policies.

- Advantages and advanced planning applications of purchasing private placement life insurance.

- Using loans to finance the purchase of a large life insurance policy.

FOREIGN NATIONALS USING U.S. LIFE INSURANCE POLICIES

For affluent foreign nationals, there are significant advantages to purchasing U.S. life insurance policies. These individuals can often readily benefit from the maturity and, therefore, better rates and often higher quality products characteristic of the U.S. life insurance market.

These life insurance policies are exclusively for international high-net-worth clients who meet the following two criteria:

 Have no U.S. ties such as property ownership.

 Have a need for large amount of life insurance, which is not available in his or her country of residence.

There are two more benefits that are appealing to many wealthy foreign nationals. They are:

- The life insurance policies are denominated in U.S. dollars and where distributions are currently exempt from U.S. tax withholdings on gains in the policy.

- When there are concerns about confidentiality.

These life insurance policies are not applicable if the wealthy individual is a U.S. citizen or legal resident with a green card. They're also inappropriate if the affluent non-U.S. citizen has financial U.S. ties such as real estate holdings, a U.S.-based trust, bank accounts, and equity interests in private businesses.

CASE STUDIES

The following are common examples where affluent foreign nationals benefit from U.S. life insurance policies.

CASE # 1 A 35-year-old South American inheritor needs US$25 million to protect an income stream going to his family. He wants to pay for the life insurance policy quickly and needs the protection for as long as he lives. It would also be useful if he can have access to the cash value in U.S. dollars.

In this case, we structured a life insurance policy to be paid up in five years with the ability to build up significant cash value. Everything is denominated in U.S. dollars and the transaction is both transparent and confidential.

CASE #

2

A 55-year-old Middle-Eastern individual has US$5 million in an account intended for his grandchildren. He wants to ensure the money is available to them without complication.

The answer was a U.S. life insurance policy with a face value of US$40 million. This way the grandchildren will get a substantial inheritance, and monies can also be accessed, if need be, from the life insurance policy via loans.

CASE #

3

A 30-year-old European third-generation business owner needs to provide guarantees for a sizable business loan. She's not interested in encumbering her assets.

The solution is a U.S. life insurance policy whose US$20 million death benefit is used as collateral. Moreover, because of the way this transaction is structured, provided she holds the policy for about fifteen years, she will be able to start getting the cost of the premium payments returned as well as have a completely paid up life insurance policy.

To get the greatest benefit from these types of life insurance policies requires some degree of ingenuity. When these types of policies are integrated with advanced planning, many more possibilities for tax mitigation are available.

Another type of policy of interest to the ultra-wealthy is private placement life insurance.

PRIVATE PLACEMENT LIFE INSURANCE

Affluent investors care about what they keep, not what they earn. For over two decades, one of the best-kept secrets in tax planning has been private placement life insurance, which makes it possible for a hedge fund investor to garner tax-free returns. Private placement life insurance is a variable universal life insurance policy that provides cash value appreciation based on a segregated investment account combined with a life insurance benefit. Private placement life insurance is designed to maximize savings while minimizing the death benefit. The investment account can be invested in tax-inefficient hedge fund strategies via an insurance dedicated account (see below).

The cost of private placement life insurance averages 1% to 1.5% of the amount invested annually. Assuming the private placement life insurance policy is purchased over three or four years, the policy owner has tax-free access to the private placement life insurance policy's value through policy loans. If held to the insured person's death, the investment account and the insurance coverage are paid out as a death benefit, free of income tax. Depending on local law and the entity that owns the policy, private placement life insurance policies allow significant creditor protection from tort, contract, and marital creditors.

Private placement life insurance policies typically require a minimum US$3 million to US$5 million investment spread out over three to four years. Gradual funding of the policy enables non-taxable loans to be taken from the policy.

Private placement life insurance policies are not liquid capital. It's shelf money that may be available to the owner if necessary, but is really intended to grow tax-free often for the benefit of future generations. Private placement life insurance is a terrific option for pre-existing multigenerational trusts.

Insurance dedicated funds. The simplest and most common way to invest in a private placement life insurance policy is through "insurance dedicated funds." An insurance dedicated fund is a hedge fund that is open only to investors who are buying the investment through a life insurance policy or an annuity product.

A major—for some—investment restriction is that the owner of a private placement life insurance policy cannot control the purchase and sale of underlying investments in the segregated account. For example, a hedge fund manager cannot form an insurance dedicated fund and purchase a policy that holds his or her own insurance dedicated fund.

This limitation should not be confused with the ability of a private placement life insurance owner to switch the funds invested in the private placement life insurance contract's investment account. If performance of one insurance dedicated fund disappoints, it is easy to request that the insurance company switch to a different and better-performing insurance dedicated fund, so long as the owner does not control the underlying investments in the new insurance dedicated fund.

Private placement life insurance and tax planning. Private placement life insurance is especially useful as a component of more complicated tax strategies. If an affluent client has a significant windfall resulting in a large infusion of ordinary income in a particular year, such as the recognition of offshore deferrals for a hedge fund manager or a large bonus for an executive or business owner, private placement life insurance, in conjunction with a charitable lead annuity trust, can offset the tax while supporting philanthropic causes including private foundations. At the end of a successful long-term charitable lead annuity trust, wealth that is significantly greater than the original contribution can pass, free of gift taxes, to children or other loved ones.

Private placement life insurance can address many cross-border tax problems faced by international families. Private placement life insurance provides a partial solution to foreign non-grantor trusts with accumulation problems, as it prevents the trust from realizing additional income on an annual basis. Private placement life insurance, or more likely a private placement annuity, can temporarily shelter non-U.S. investments from the U.S. tax system for a foreign national who intends to return to his or her home country eventually, but who is assuming a post in the U.S., and therefore, will be a tax resident in the U.S. and temporarily subject to U.S. income tax on worldwide income.

In sum, private placement life insurance is income tax efficient while providing the owner with tax-free access to the policy cash values. With proper planning, the cash value appreciation and insurance coverage can also escape gift, estate, and additional taxes. It can be structured to provide world-class creditor protection.

Private placement life insurance is a legitimate tool for bright-line sophisticated tax planning. It's a perfect solution for patient investors who desire exposure to tax-inefficient hedge funds without paying confiscatory income taxes.

CASE STUDIES

The following are two examples where private placement life insurance proved quite useful.

CASE # 1 An affluent client sets up a non-grantor trust for the benefit of her children and funded it with a US$5 million gift. The trustee invested the gifted funds in hedge funds. Unfortunately, the trust would have to pay taxes at a rate of almost 50% on the annual earnings because of the increased tax rates that came into effect in the U.S. on January 1, 2013 with the passing of The American Taxpayer Relief Act. Paying the high tax rates on the trust's earning each year will significantly hamper the growth of the assets for the children.

By investing the US$5 million private placement life insurance, the trustee can still invest in hedge funds, receive tax deferred growth on the underlying hedge fund earnings, and provide a US$20 million tax free death benefit for the children.

CASE # 2 A successful hedge fund manager has to bring back to the United States US$50 million in offshore hedge fund deferrals, which will be taxed at ordinary income tax rates. Instead of losing almost 50% of the offshore deferrals to taxes, he contributes them to a charitable lead annuity trust. The charitable lead annuity trust contribution will give him an offsetting charitable tax deduction, which almost eliminates the income taxes due from the offshore deferrals that are due.

Because the policy earnings grow tax deferred, there are no annual income taxes due on the earnings in the policy. In this case, the hedge fund manager offsets his income taxes by donating to the charitable lead annuity trust, gives money to charity, gets a tax deferral of all investment earnings, and passes the funds to his heirs income and estate tax free.

The attractions of private placement life insurance are the investment options—hedge funds—combined with the tax-efficiency of life insurance. Aside from the direct advantages, private placement life insurance, as shown, can be an instrumental component of complex advanced planning.

We've been addressing two variations of life insurance policies. Another consideration for the ultra-wealthy is how to best pay for life insurance. There are many ways this can be accomplished such as composite cross-border arbitrage strategies, the use of offsetting derivatives, and premium financing. The last possibility is the easiest to implement and the one we'll now discuss.

PREMIUM FINANCING

The essence of premium financing as the term suggests is where the affluent individual takes out a loan to pay for his or her life insurance policy. There are a number of reasons this can be a wise financial move including:

- Permanent life insurance policies have a cash surrender value that can provide collateral for a secured loan.

- There are available life insurance policies offering attractive options for the policy cash value that can diversify the client's investment portfolio and outperform the cost of financing premiums.

- It enables the acquisition of higher face values when there are cash flow concerns.

- In the U.S., where the annual premium exceeds the annual gift tax exclusion for irrevocable trusts, premium financing outlays can be structured to qualify for the annual gift tax exclusion.

The advantages of borrowing life insurance premiums are tangible and valuable. This payment strategy can potentially increase a wealthy person's net worth modestly during his or her lifetime and increase the after-tax estate substantially after death. Premium financing also creates the flexibility to adjust the amount of leverage built into the life insurance policy when initially purchased and periodically over time.

The structure of a typical transaction. Although each premium financing transaction is customized, the basic terms and techniques are somewhat standard as follows:

- The loan typically is non-recourse-secured by the life insurance policy's cash value and a letter of credit equal to any shortfall between loan principal and cash value.

- The policy is permanent life insurance in which coverage is guaranteed for life or to a very high age (e.g., 121 years old).

- The loan interest is a floating rate typically tied to the 12-month LIBOR plus a spread.

- A loan arrangement fee ranges from 1% to about 1.25% depending on loan size, and it can be capitalized into loan principal.

Premium financing works best when the life insurance policy has the potential to grow cash value at higher rates than the cost of financing. With interest rates where they're currently residing, it's—relatively speaking—a good time to consider this approach.

Exiting the loan. In evaluating a proposed transaction, affluent individuals should understand the common strategies for exiting a premium financing arrangement. In addition to paying off the loan, the options include:

- Having the trust or estate pay off the loan after death using insurance proceeds.

- Surrendering the contract and using its cash value to pay off the loan.

- Restructuring the loan.

- Using a combination of personal assets and policy withdrawals or policy loans to pay off the premium finance loan.

Premium financing arrangements normally do not include loan prepayment fees. Therefore, the ultra-wealthy client can "dial down" leverage by paying off loan principal whenever liquidity is available and the differential makes economic sense.

CASE STUDIES

The following two case studies show how premium financing can be an effective way to mitigate the cost of life insurance policy premiums.

CASE # 1 A 54-year-old second-generation real estate developer had a need for US$100 million of life insurance to fund estate taxes. Most of his cash assets were tied up in his properties. The annual premium to pay the policy outright was a little more than US$1.8 million per year for his lifetime for a level death benefit policy. On top of that, the client did not have enough annual exclusion (gifting) beneficiaries so he would have to pay additional gift taxes on the premiums being paid to the trust that would own the policy.

Since the developer was used to leverage as he had bought so many of his properties that way, we looked into a premium finance arrangement. The developer's trust, which would own the policy, was able to borrow the policy premiums from a third party lender. He funded the policy at high levels in order for it to be self-supporting after seven to ten years. Since the policy would be funded at very high levels, the cash value would collateralize most of the loan. The developer would post collateral for any shortfall between the policy cash value and the loan balance. The annual interest charged on the loan could be paid annually or accrued into the loan. This gave him a lot of flexibility for cash flow management.

CASE # 2 A husband and wife in their mid-60's worth US$90 million were updating their estate plan. They wanted US$25 million of life insurance for estate tax purposes. The premiums for the coverage were just under US$400,000 annually. The couple did not want to disturb their existing investment portfolio as they were achieving superior returns and had been for a while.

They chose a premium finance arrangement to fund the annual premiums for the second-to-die policy. Under the premium finance arrangement, the policy would be funded at a high level for seven years with the policy's cash value providing most of the collateral for the loan. The shortfall was posted by one of the children's trusts, which was already holding significant assets. The couple chose to pay the interest annually through gifting. An advantage of the program would allow the loan to be repaid using policy cash values in the future. This gave the couple the ability to fund their life insurance at a significant discount as well as preserve their investments.

Premium financing is only a viable and cost-effective way to buy life insurance in very specific circumstances. There are many times when it makes sense for the ultra-wealthy provided the life insurance policies are carefully monitored so that adjustments can be made when needed.

CONCLUSIONS

Life insurance is a very versatile product that can deliver tremendous results when employed properly. It can be a critical component of an array of advanced planning strategies capitalizing on its tax-efficiencies and other advantages inherent in the product. Furthermore, there are a variety of ways to address paying life insurance premiums with premium financing being one example.

It's important to emphasize that life insurance is only one funding alternative, among a handful, when it comes to advanced planning strategies. While it can prove very advantageous for the ultra-wealthy, all alternatives should always be considered and evaluated based on the particular affluent individual's situation, preferences, and needs.

Frank W. Seneco is president of Seneco & Associates, Inc. (www.seneco.com). He's an internationally recognized authority on the use of advanced planning strategies incorporating life insurance. He works with the ultra-wealthy and family offices designing bespoke tax and compensation solutions.

Evan Jehle is a partner at Flynn Family Office Solutions (www.flynnfamilyoffice.com). As an advanced planning and technical specialist, he brings state-of-the-art tax and financial strategies to the firm's high net-worth clients including family offices, celebrities and hedge fund general partners.

17

CONNECTED CARE FOR THE HIGH-NET-WORTH FAMILY: MILLENNIALS WILL LEAD THE WAY

by Daniel Carlin, M.D.

AS EVERYONE KNOWS, HEALTHCARE IS CHANGING.

Across the globe, demographic and economic pressures are forcing families to rethink how they will access quality medical care in the future. Historically, their solutions focused on comprehensive health insurance with the goal of providing the means to pay for good care. This model assumed good medicine was easily available, but with an ever-contracting physician base, the explosive growth of retirees, and limited funds to pay for their healthcare, good medicine made available to everyone is no longer a valid assumption.

Part of the problem is that good medicine is composed of both art and science. This is problematic, as the scalable "one model fits all" paradigm found in most other industries does not apply well in medicine. Physician skills such as interpersonal communication and bedside manner are critical to accurate diagnosis (and thus effective treatment), but are not easily evaluated. The exception is simple chronic disease states like hypertension and diabetes, where hard numbers (blood pressure and serum glucose) enable more scalable data-driven care models.

The situation is compounded by the heterogeneous nature of patient populations. Across cultures and geographic regions, how people interpret and relate their health concerns varies greatly. Nowhere is this difference more notable than between generations. In contrast to their kids, baby boomers are comfortable with one-on-one conversation, intimate and personal, with their doctor. This conversation forms the basis of clinical information gathering and is the most efficient approach for accurate diagnosis.

Unfortunately, this conversational approach may not be enough in some cases, and hard data (lab numbers/exam results) is then pursued. It is in this latter data-centric step where the Millennials' approach is superior to their parents. Having been raised in the world of almost complete connectivity, Millennials look to the clever smartphone app or the intelligent database tool to solve the problem of the moment, whether it is connecting with food delivery (e.g., Grub Hub) or blood pressure management (e.g., Withings).

The prediction is that the future winners in healthcare will succeed by combining the sensibility of both generations into a single common-sense platform integrating the best of the personal communication with easy and relevant personal health data tracking.

There is an urgency to make this happen soon. Though well intentioned, the Affordable Care Act (a.k.a. Obamacare) has extended the U.S.'s dysfunctional third-party payment model to an additional 40 million patients. The third party/insurance paradigm started in the 1960s (a decade of unrelenting prosperity) and was focused on providing clients with the means to pay for new and expensive crisis care interventions (chemotherapy, cardiac bypass surgery, etc). Fast forward 50 years, the U.S. now has per capita the most expensive healthcare in the world while ranking a distant 37th in citizen longevity. Along the way, the fiscal resources devoted to primary and preventive care dwindled to a point that there has been over the last decade a net egress of thousands of practicing primary care physicians, and their empty offices are not being staffed with fresh graduates eager to take their place.

For the affluent family, the historical plan for good health care has composed of being a major donor or board member of their local hospital. Barring that, the family would often have a long-term relationship with a senior internist who could meet their need for flexible hours and weekend availability. This kind of relationship became more formalized with the advent of concierge medicine, wherein the doctor was paid an annual retainer to provide rapid phone call returns and facilitated appointments. The quality range among concierge physicians is generally good, though the range of their expertise, referral relationships, and professional influence is limited to their base hospital and not extensible beyond their hometown. For a high-net-worth family, this is a good, but only a partial solution for two reasons: The local concierge MD is not set up to care for them while traveling, and for a serious issues like cancer or spinal injury, the best specialist might not be within their referral network.

With regard to accessing hospital-based resources, the situation is likely to be quite challenging in the future. This problem may or may not be made worse by Obamacare, but there is an inescapable demographic reality coming. Ten thousand men and women turn

65 each day becoming both Medicare eligible and joining the ranks of those who will, based purely on age, need serious healthcare services. By 2025, there will be 30 million of them, having spent little effort on personal prevention or wellness, and thus will dispro-portionately occupy the critical care units, cardiac care units, and general medicine hos-pital beds.

This dire situation is already a daily reality in most of our inner cities and is a window on what is to come. Every emergency physician in practice will affirm that having too many patients and too few primary care doctors is a dangerous combination creating chronic emergency room overload, near-constant bed shortages, and a burned out nursing and support staff.

STAYING HEALTHY

Despite all of the complex (and often unrealistic) solutions being put forth, there is actu-ally a simple effective strategy to address this risk: Stay healthy enough to avoid the emergency room and the hospital as long as possible. In short, keep preventable illness at bay for as long as you can. This strategy is not confined just to the US, but to every country where people want to live longer, and good hospital-based healthcare may be in short supply. Ironically, when followed to fruition, the vast majority of us will also live longer, more productive and healthier lives. The key change is to engage in the active pursuit of effective prevention.

There's further good news. Prevention is a science, and that science is growing in leaps and bounds. The only problem is that some of the "science" in prevention is not true science at all. Some of the "miracle breakthroughs" are pure hype, even quackery. On the credible side, there have been major advances with predictive biomarkers in cardiovas-cular disease, circulating tumor-specific protein markers, and genetic patterns associated with future risk for common cancers.

On the discreditable side, there are too many options to name. If the practice/cure is endorsed by celebrity (usually past their prime), coupled with unverified research in another country or specifically marketed through the statement, "the miracle breakthrough doctors don't want you to know about," chances are good that it is a sham.

A simpler and vastly more promising trend in prevention is the concept of planned longev-ity. Though still nascent as a discipline, the idea of creating a formal calendared plan to capture and track key invalid biometric data and manage them to a determined goal is powerful. Neither is it complex. The numbers to track include:

- Blood pressure.

- Cholesterol/lipids.

- Body mass index/weight.

- Exercise tolerance.

- Inflammatory biomarkers.

- Genetic risk markers.

The most effective of these plans will also place a strong emphasis on formal nutrition and exercise programs. Ultimately, the longevity plan will become a highly personalized map on each person integrating their unique risks and tracking their personal biometric data to create the greatest chance for the longest possible active life.

CONTINUOUSLY CONNECTED CARE

Millennials have a huge role to play in the maturation of this kind of planned longevity. Their propensity to include personal connectivity and data driven apps in their life skills is a good fit. Using a smartphone as the enabling technology, there are already thousands of wellness apps covering everything from mood scoring, calorie consumption, and exercise tolerance. In a not-so-distant day, the best of the smartphone apps will be intelligently combined and connected with a physician care team to support the longevity plan and deliver real-time care wherever the patient might be.

At fruition, this new model of "continuously connected care" will solve a lot of the problems currently facing conventional health care. Among the most important solutions will be:

- Restoration of physician access.

- Continuity of personal medical information.

- Effective utilization of high-level specialist and hospital resources.

- Active disease-free longevity.

In execution, continuously connected care looks a lot like a medical "mission-control" whose operations host:

- A licensed physician to relate a problem/interpret the situation.

- Reception and interpretation of personal monitoring data
  (e.g., blood pressure, heart rhythm).

- Easy access to an ongoing "report card" display of the patient's progress.

- Complete continuity of personal medical records.

- Care team architecture capable of matching "right problem to
  right provider" quickly.

While the concept of a medical mission control is relatively new among humans, there are two precedent models succeeding in two different but related fields: dairy farming and automotive maintenance.

For more than 20 years, U.S. Department of Agriculture has required every cow's health and activity to be tracked from birth to death. As part of a national registry, every cow born in the US is issued a unique identifier (recently tied to an radio frequency identification tag placed on their ear) connecting that cow to every one of its health events, from immunizations to geographic range to milk quality to death. This comprehensive approach to cow wellness came about as the solution to preventing Mad Cow disease, and it remains an ongoing success story.

On the automotive front, in 1996 General Motors launched OnStar: a vehicle-enabled communication tool to support planned maintenance, driver safety, and concierge support services. In their GM car, a driver can call an OnStar representative and receive immediate counsel on an automotive problem or logistical issue. The system can also retrieve the vehicle's maintenance records and even unlock or start the car should the driver forget the keys. Not surprisingly, vehicles with active OnStar users last longer and have a higher resale value than those with less involved drivers. For both cows and GM cars, the continuously connected care model has proved a huge success with a verifiable and positive return on investment.

With affluent Millennials supporting this healthcare evolution for the benefit of their parents, connected care will happen even faster and not just for the benefit of longer-lived parents. Thanks to a generational sensibility tying personal investment to social good, Millennials are aggressively pursuing business opportunities in the connected care space. The early winners are companies enabling faster patient appointments (e.g., ZocDoc) and simple medical questions (e.g., Health Tap), and though these firms do not yet include actual care delivery, it is only a matter of time until companies engage this challenge and fulfill this pressing need.

CONCLUSION

Right now, two people are having a conversation about how to change the world of healthcare. One is a doctor and the other is a Millennial. The doctor stresses that good medicine is the art of listening long enough to reduce a story to a recognizable pattern. The Millennial affirms this, and extends the idea that pattern is data, and there's more to come if they can build the system to harvest and process it into real clinical care.

The doctor and the Millennial go back and forth in an earnest, sometime fractious exchange. The only thing they can immediately agree on is that time is running short to find the solution. They also agree that whoever actually fixes this problem might also be launching the next age of medicine.

Change is coming to healthcare along with some very large and serious problems. Connected care, in all of its permutations and driven by Millennials, will be a huge part of the solution set.

Daniel Carlin M.D. is the founder and CEO of WorldClinic (www.WorldClinic.com), the leading concierge healthcare firm pioneering connected care. Dan is an internationally acclaimed expert in the use of personal technologies to deliver immediate effective medical care on an anytime/anywhere basis. WorldClinic serves the healthcare needs of executives, individuals and families, and performers and athletes.

CHAPTER

18

COMBATING PROFESSIONAL CRIMINALS

by Andrew J. O'Connell & Russ Alan Prince

ONE OF THE MORE PRESSING CONCERNS of a
majority of the ultra-wealthy is the well being of themselves and their loved ones.
Along the same lines, they're very concerned about identity theft and ensuring
their confidential information remains confidential. To a lesser degree, the
ultra-wealthy are uneasy about their property being stolen or damaged.
With respect to ultra-wealthy inheritors, these issues are discussed in
Chapter 8: Critical Lifestyle Services.

These worries are, first of all, quite rationale. Moreover, they're certainly not
restricted to the ultra-wealthy. By many criteria, although people are safer than
ever before, these issues are very real problems and anyone can be a victim.

The decision as to what actions to take—what security solutions to employ—by the ultra-wealthy, and anyone else for that matter, is a function of their level of concern and the possible consequences that are likely to befall them. The following equation places this in perspective:

 **NEED FOR A SECURITY SOLUTION** = Probability of incident **X** Severity of incident

Looking at the elements, you need to project the likelihood of an incident occurring. There is a range of possible things that can go wrong such as:

- You or a loved one is kidnapped.

- Your identity is stolen and exploited.

- Unscrupulous investment advisors victimize you.

- Your personal and medical records are hacked.

- Your home is burglarized.

Most incidents including these ones are low probability occurrences. On the other hand, some incidents if they were to happen can prove devastating. Just think about someone stealing your family's medical records and the possible repercussions, or you've invested a sizeable sum with a hedge fund manager who has stellar credentials and an even better track record who just happens to be running a Ponzi scheme. When it comes to selecting security solutions, you need to balance out the chance of something bad happening with how devastating it can be.

What's important to understand is that the ultra-wealthy on one level are no more a target than anyone else. But on another level, they're more a target than the less affluent, and this unfortunate situation is only intensifying. Accordingly, there are actions that you can take to mitigate threats.

Aside from proactively addressing the possibility of severe incidents, the ultra-wealthy can take offensive actions. After being victimized, you most assuredly have the option to take steps to rectify the situation. Again, the ability to take offensive action is not restricted to the ultra-wealthy, but they often have greater means and motivation to take action.

How you wisely go about dealing with security concerns and incidents is often decided, in part, by the way you think about predators. For instructional purposes, let's consider a very simple criminal typology.

TWO TYPES OF CRIMINALS

Let's say criminals fall into one of two categories—amateurs and professionals. As noted, this bipolar, very one-dimensional distinction is being used to educate and make a point. The reality is that there's a wide spectrum upon which criminals—amateurs and professionals—lie. Still, thinking in terms of these two categories, we can define each type based on a number of core characteristics (Exhibit 18.1).

EXHIBIT 18.1 Two Types of Criminals

CHARACTERISTICS	AMATEUR CRIMINALS	PROFESSIONAL CRIMINALS
Sophistication	Low	Medium to High
Resourcefulness	Low	High
Impulsivity	High	Low
Operational flexibility	Medium	High

Amateur criminals are inclined to be impulsive. They see what they construe to be an opportunity and take action almost reflexively. There's often little in the way of planning and preparation, which also means they do not anticipate complications resulting in limited (if any) backup alternatives. Amateur criminals predominately operate with relative few resources. They're rarely clever or ingenious when it comes to any planning they actually do or when they execute their crimes.

Professional criminals, by our definition, are more often than not sophisticated. They tend to carefully and precisely develop plans for their crimes and execute them with precision. This also means they have backup plans, as it's the norm for actions to not to go as they anticipate or prefer. In addition, professional criminals are able to tap an array of resources to use in their illegal activities.

THE LOGIC OF THINKING THE PREDATOR IS A PROFESSIONAL CRIMINAL

Based on this conceptual duality, professional criminals are likely to target the ultra-wealthy as opposed to those who are less affluent. The reasoning for this is simple: Professional criminals make risk/return decisions. If they're going to gamble on going to prison, the rewards for their efforts should be compensatory. In contrast, amateur criminals are likely to target anyone or any firm where they see some upside tending to neglect doing anything resembling a cost/benefit analysis.

For the ultra-wealthy, it proves to be wise and advantageous to think in terms of combating professional criminals. These predators are most likely to explicitly target them. Furthermore, they have a much higher chance of being successful compared to amateur criminals.

By operating as if professional criminals are the predators and taking appropriate actions, doing so will readily dissuade amateur criminals from pursuing you. While the affluence of a particular ultra-wealthy family is extraordinarily attractive to amateur criminals, the actions that protect the very rich are regularly an exponentially greater deterrent to them. At the same time, the ultra-wealthy can access significant resources to deal with professional criminals after being victimized. These same resources tend to easily overwhelm amateur criminals.

SHIFTING ATTENTION

In many ways, the best defense against the professional criminals is to become a conundrum with diverse and powerful battlements in place. Put another way, an optimal shielding strategy for dealing with professional criminals is to shift attention away from yourself, your loved ones, and your business interests. By hardening the vulnerabilities in your world and simultaneously fostering systematic confusion when it comes to information concerning you and those you care deeply about, you and all you hold dear become an increasingly less appealing target to professional criminals.

Let's be clear. There's no way to erect physical, technological, and operational barriers to eliminate every conceivable threat. Even if you could afford it, you need not create and live in an impervious domed enclave replete with all the latest security technology and safeguarded by squadron of drones armed with hellfire missiles. It's not a matter of expense; it's a matter of practicality.

Even a fortress mentality coupled with the wealth to build the fortress cannot possibly eradicate all potential threats. If you're dealing with a true creative psychopathic criminal mastermind, for example, then nothing you do will likely stop him or her. It's to his or her advantage being a completely amoral criminal genius. Thankfully, these brilliantly cunning sinister architects of bedlam are exceedingly more common in thrillers than in real life.

What you're focused on accomplishing is making your world a much more difficult target for professional criminals. Professional criminals are going to research you and your situation. If they conclude you're a difficult target compared to others in your cohort, then they'll pass on you in favor of one of your peers.

There are many ways to harden the vulnerabilities in your world. Some of them are focused on technology so as to avoid data and identity theft. Some of them are focused on education, such as how to protect yourself against being hacked and how to deal with an attacker when you have no other options (see *Chapter 19: Taking Matters Into Their Own Hands*). Then there are many ways to create protective environments including safe rooms and the use of close protection personnel.

It's also wise to sow confusion in the minds of professional criminals. Before they act, professional criminals will conduct research on your world. If they cannot get access to the information they need, they're very inclined to move onto someone else. If there's a lot of information about you in the public domain, by mudding the waters you can make yourself a less appealing target. For example, if your home address is easily accessible on the Internet, there's always the option of having multiple home addresses available to anyone using the Internet to find where you live even if you reside at only one location.

What makes the judicious enhancement of your defensives including fostering perplexity such a powerful defensive strategy against professional criminals is that, among the ultra-wealthy, it's fairly uncommon. Ironically, we find that while the majority of the ultra-wealthy are intellectually aware of the many potential security disasters they face, until something happens to them or people they know fairly well, viscerally they're often not anxious enough to take action. And, they'll regularly not take proactive actions to protect themselves or other people who are important to them or their corporate interests until something has gone painfully wrong.

By shifting the attention of professional criminals away from your world, they will almost unerringly redirect their nefarious schemes to one of your peers who has failed to make the effort to adequately protect himself. By taking this defensive approach, you not only are likely to thwart professional criminals, but most probably, the amateurs don't have a chance.

FINDING ANSWERS

Even if you do an excellent job of solidifying the exposures in your world and confounding a criminal's ability to dissect your life, professional criminals might still target you. What they expect to gain offsets the risks involved—even the heightened risks.

It's important to remember that committing a crime and getting away with it are two very different things. Just ask the many people sitting in prison.

After many criminal acts, for the ultra-wealthy the ofttimes preferred course of action is to find out precisely what happened and seek appropriate redress. It's very important to understand, what were the faults in your security that were exploited? This information is critical as you will likely want to take actions to make certain you're not confronted with the same horrid problem ever again.

In some ways, by finding the answers after an incident, you're able to close the barn door after the horse has left. For some people this would be a meaningless exercise. However, for the ultra-wealthy it's usually very valuable. Yes, you're closing the barn door after the horse has left, but very likely in your world, the barn is full of other horses. At the same time, by seeking and finding answers, you're working ardently to find the horse that got out and bring it home.

When you find the answers you need, you're positioned to initiate corrective actions. The definition of "corrective action" is a function of the crime. If your house was burgled, for example, and some very expensive fine art was stolen, redress is probably defined as the return of the artwork and prison time for the thieves. Another example is if you're being blackmailed, redress is eliminating the threat and ensuring the blackmailer is handed over to the proper authorities.

Principally, the way you find answers is by conducting investigations. The nature of the investigations—the level of effort and scope of work—is determined by the complexity and severity of the incident. In general, the two big questions you're looking to answer are "how?" and "why?" otherwise referred to as "method" and "motive."

As with the strategy of shifting attention, finding answers is usually monumentally easier when it comes to amateur criminals. Their lack of sophistication and finesse generally makes it very easy to source them and makes it many times much easier to correct the damage they caused.

PROFESSIONAL CRIMINALS TARGETING THE BUSINESS INTERESTS OF THE ULTRA-WEALTHY

When it comes to the ultra-wealthy, there's regularly more at risk than themselves: the people they care about and their personal property. It's normative for their business endeavors to also be targeted by professional criminals.

Family offices (see *Chapter 20: The Family Office Solution*), for example, because of the fact they're booming in numbers as well as the wealth they control, are increasingly in the cross hairs of professional criminals. While the overall situation is improving, many family offices badly leak proprietary information making the family office itself, and the ultra-wealthy families involved, a relatively easy target for professional criminals.

Professional criminals are also in myriad ways targeting the operating business ultra-wealthy families are running. Experienced con artists, for example, can often exploit the family/business dynamics. Professional criminals without question are not just targeting the enterprises of the ultra-wealthy. They'll just as easily target any company they believe will pay off respectfully well considering failure is likely to equal incarceration.

The very same strategies—shifting attention and finding answers—are applicable and viable when it comes to businesses as the ultra-wealthy as individuals. Without question, there are many tactical differences, but the underlying thinking and approach remains the same. It's also important to note that nowadays, the tactical differences between the ultra-wealthy and corporations are many times not that far apart.

CONCLUSIONS

This admittedly modest look at dealing with a particular kind of predator illuminates two powerful strategies to protecting the people and things that matter to you as well as what actions need to be taken after being victimized. There are many, many more permutations you might need to address to effectively deal with criminals and potentially devastating situations such as law suits, governmental inquiries, natural disasters, terrorists, travel to "hot spots," and the list goes on and on.

For many of the ultra-wealthy, these two strategies should be seriously considered. One, the greatest ability to ensure the safety of you and yours is to be proactive. Two, being able to make decidedly constructive and extremely effective counter-moves after an incident is by deftly understanding the nature of the events and the mind-set and methodologies of the predators. By knowing how criminals regularly think and act, there are actions you can take to mitigate potential threats and effectually address incidents after the fact.

Having all the security "tools" in the world is useless unless they can be employed at the right time and the right way. We find that being insightful and attuned to the criminal's psychology, coupled with state-of-the-art family and business security solutions, it's very possible to dramatically and successfully combat professional criminals.

Andrew J. O'Connell is the Chief Executive Officer of Guidepost Solutions LLC (www.guidepostsolutions.com). He is a former federal prosecutor and federal agent. He provides expert investigative and security consulting services and advice to companies, individuals, and their counsel to solve problems, advance business opportunities, mitigate risks, and resolve disputes. He oversees and conducts private investigations and security assessments throughout the United States and the world.

CHAPTER 19

TAKING MATTERS
INTO THEIR OWN HANDS

by George Chaber & Jerry D. Prince

WHEN IT COMES to the exceptionally wealthy protecting themselves and their loved ones, the logical set of actions is to carefully evaluate their situations and install the appropriate safeguards. This regularly entails addressing the physical security of their homes and other properties such as planes and boats. It may very well include the use of top-flight executive protection personnel. Working with talented professionals to put the proper safeguards in place is smart, judicious, and—by most any criteria—highly cost-effective.

As many very wealthy individuals prefer not to live encased in a protective bubble, there are times all these well conceived and executed precautions are not in use. In effect, they're out of the security zone and potentially quite vulnerable. A percentage of these extremely affluent individuals still want to know they'll be safe in that they can protect themselves and their loved ones in dire situations.

For other wealthy individuals, being completely dependent on others for their safety and the safety of their families, is an anathema. While there are certainly times when it's intelligent to turn to security professionals; nevertheless, they themselves want to know that they can deal with certain extreme conditions.

These wealthy individuals represent a small but slowly growing segment of the high-net-worth population. For them and their families, we developed an intense, compact, highly effective self-defense methodology we refer to as extreme personal defense—XPD for short.

PROTECTION THROUGH DESTRUCTION

XPD is all about **crippling your attacker's ability to harm you or the ones you care about when no other option is available.** The express and clear aim of XPD is to empower students of the program with the mental fortitude and the technical ability to devastate, obliterate, and decimate an assailant. When the situation is indeed exceedingly desperate, killing an attacker is certainly a possibility.

For some people, this sounds a little over the edge. Because of the potency of XPD, we've noticed that words like "insane," "psycho," and f**king nuts" have been used to describe it. However, most people come around to our way of thinking when they understand the highly restricted times XPD is applicable.

Consider the following examples. Which ones do you think would be good times for you to know XPD?

SCENARIO 1

With your spouse and two toddlers, you're going to have a picnic at a park. You ride over to the neighborhood park and see that many other families had the same idea. As you exit your car, a couple of teenagers more than twenty feet away start harassing you. They're making lewd and disgusting comments.
WHAT DO YOU DO?

SCENARIO 2

You've parked your car in an office-building garage. As you head for the garage exit to go to a late afternoon meeting, a thief with a fairly large knife stops you and demands you hand over your money and any other valuables.
WHAT DO YOU DO?

SCENARIO 3

Two men grab you as you're about to enter your house. One of them is holding a knife, and he tells you they're going inside where your spouse and toddler are. He says they're going to have a party, and if you do just what he says, you, your spouse, and your kid won't get cut too badly.
WHAT DO YOU DO?

What would you do? Which scenario is potentially a good time to be proficient with XPD?

Unless the situation quickly escalates dramatically, you probably don't need to do anything in Scenario #1. There are people all around and the teenagers are being obnoxious teenagers. If they don't do anything else but mouth off, they're not a threat.

In Scenario #2, the stakes are raised. The best course of action is to hand over your valuables. You can always replace the valuables. Conflict should be avoided whenever possible.

XPD is only potentially applicable in Scenario #3, and only if you absolutely believe that the two men who grabbed you are serious threats to you and your family. If you indeed ardently believe these two men are dangerous to the lives of you and your loved ones, when they're both right next to you, and you alone, is the best time to eliminate the threat.

XPD is an intensely destructive form of self-defense and should only be employed when there are **absolutely no other options available to you**. These are the times when not defending yourself or the people you care deeply about would unquestionably result in horrible things happening to you or them. XPD is for dealing with absolute worst-case family safety situations.

UP CLOSE AND VERY PERSONAL

Returning to Scenario #3, if you're going to fight back, doing so right outside your house when your assailants are right next to you is often the most opportune moment. If they were to get into your house and bring your family into the conflict, your options decrease exponentially as your attackers are now likely to be out of immediate reach, and there are your loved ones you have to consider in taking any action.

There certainly are lots of implicit assumptions in this scenario. Nevertheless, when you're confident it's life or death, or grave injury to you or loves ones, and you see no other viable solutions, then it's time to take action. Then XPD may very well make sense.

A key reason the moment outside your house in Scenario #3 is so opportune is because your assailants were both right next to you. XPD is all about disabling attackers who are in close proximity.

In the material arts, there are basically three ranges—close range, mid-range, and far range. XPD is only for dealing with attackers in close range. It's not about squaring off against an opponent, which is more evident in mid-range and a given in far range. Those are fights where both sides know it's a fight. XPD is about you doing severe damage or worse to your assailants before they have any idea they're possibly fighting for their own lives. This requires your assaulters to be less than an arm's length away.

XPD is derived from other martial arts with the recognition that students need to learn powerful practical defense techniques fairly quickly. The techniques that comprise XPD were drawn from a variety of styles such as Silat and Pagamut with a smattering of Jeet Kune Do. It even integrates a few highly destructive techniques from some more esoteric martial arts such as Dim Mak. All the techniques were carefully chosen and then significantly modified for the immediacy of the potential confrontations and for quick mastery.

TACTICAL ADVANTAGES

XPD is pragmatic. It's about getting results when your back is against the wall: when you've concluded you have no other choice. XPD has three major tactical advantages, which make it so effective:

- Combat mindfulness.

- Surprise and speed.

- Strategic striking.

Let's now consider each of these tactical advantages.

Combat mindfulness. You need to be actively aware and observant of the threat while your fears are very present but not disabling. Being able to judge the level of danger and your options requires a keen understanding of what is going on around you and what might happen.

Verbal aggression as evidenced by the teenagers in Scenario #1 is not a reason to ever hurt someone. The danger from the teenagers who are a distance away is likely to be minimal, if at all. Unless a person has a gun or is close to you, they are unlikely to be able to hurt you or the people you're with.

In Scenario #2 the danger is much greater. The thief is close and armed with a large knife. There's certainly the potential for you to be hurt and even killed. But there's a viable option. You can acquiesce to the thief's demands. Avoiding any physical confrontation is always the best course of action.

The third scenario is where you've determined there's a very real and very dangerous threat to yourself and your loved ones. You've determined that not using XPD will likely result in you or your family being at a minimum very badly hurt. You're extremely scared and objectively understand the danger you, your spouse, and child are in. Being so very scared tells you that this is the time you're most likely to ensure their safety as well as your own.

What's essential to the ability to use XPD is the mental preparedness to take action. Many times the hardest decision is the decision to act. "Pulling the trigger," which means turning yourself into a deadly weapon, may be one of the most difficult choices you'll ever have to make. Moreover, once you "pulled the trigger," you cannot go back. Halfway measures can prove more deleterious than having done nothing. If your attackers are not completely debilitated, you hurting them may only make the situation worse for you and your loved ones.

There are other cognitive aspects to combat mindfulness. What's important to recognize is that your mind-set, when confronted with attackers in these types of severe situations, is THE most important determining factor to the survival of yourself and your loved ones. Your ability to think clearly enough—as cool, calm and collected when truly threatened is only in the movies—to evaluate the situation and wisely choose when and how to fight back.

Surprise and speed. Whenever possible the objective is to assertively respond to your assailants when they're not ready. Their mistaken confidence often results in a lack of vigilance making it much easier for you to defend yourself and loved ones.

The two assailants in Scenario #3 most likely believe they're in total control, that they had the upper hand. They're holding you and they have the knife. For your benefit, this is what you want them to think. Additionally, if you can convey that you're paralyzed and despondent out of fear—you're scared, but you have presence of mind—you're actually lowering their defenses making it easier for you to take command of the situation.

It's helpful to be able to accentuate your one-down position, which lasts up until the split-second you strike. The more messages—verbal and non-verbal—you send saying you're in their power, the easier it will be to walk away unharmed. Generally, this is a matter of playing up your fear and weakness.

When you do take action, you're doing so quickly. Using XPD to incapacitate your assailants will usually take less than a minute. Everything happens fast as you go on automatic pilot. This ensures your attackers have no time to recover thereby eliminating them as a threat.

Strategic strikes. Hammering certain parts of the body in particular ways can be exceedingly destructive. As the goal of XPD is to enable you to quickly and seriously disable your attacker, there are places on a person's body to hit for maximum results. You want to strike the parts of your attacker's body that are most vulnerable to sudden trauma.

Optimally, each strike is a combination of a type of hit to a particular target. The proper strike to the proper target produces the most damage. It's important to note that you can hit a target with various strikes depending on the way you and your attacker are positioned (Exhibit 19.1). Some of the combinations are exceedingly powerful, while other combinations are just very powerful. Either way, they're designed to debilitate an attacker expeditiously.

EXHIBIT 19.1 Examples From the Strategic Strike Grid

TARGET	FINGERS	HAND	ELBOW	KNEE
Eyes	✔			
Throat	✔	✔		
Temple		✔	✔	
Kidney		✔	✔	
Spine		✔	✔	
Groin				✔

What's very useful about XPD is that even when the combination is mismatched—the wrong strike with the wrong target—the strike still usually does the job without a problem. In those few messy minutes when you're defending yourself by employing XPD, even getting them somewhat wrong will enable you to incapacitate your assailants.

To be effective, these techniques require they become automatic. In the martial arts this is referred to as "muscle memory." Once you decide to act, you don't have to think about your movements, as they'll happen automatically. Thus, XPD is about mastering a few hyper-harmful techniques, which requires extensive rehearsals.

THE RULE OF THREE

Part of "muscle memory" that is core to XPD is what we call the "Rule of Three." It's very important to make sure that when assaulted, the attacker is unable to in any way be able to cause you serious harm. At the same time, it's not uncommon for even a perfectly placed strike to not totally disable an attacker. Thus, the "Rule of Three."

In XPD students learn combination attacks. For the most part, strategically striking three times in a row will likely ensure your attacker is incapable of doing harm including chasing you as you get help. Interestingly, there are likely to be times—many times—when a XPD practitioner will be only able to strike twice or even once before the attacker is rendered harmless. In some circumstances, more strikes will be necessary. Being able to reflexively strike three or more times is part and parcel of the program.

Commonly, there's a rhythm to the strikes. One common patter is "strike-strike-pause-strike." Here, after determining fighting back is the only viable option, you hit a target location, followed immediately by hitting another target location—all in a fluid progression. Then you take a tiny moment to evaluate the state of the attacker. In that tiny moment of assessment, you can decide if another strike is warranted, and if so, based on body mechanics, where to strike.

Strategic striking combinations are not set in stone. They're a function of the particular situation and a product of the extensive practice that forms "muscle memory." What's important to realize is that the ability to deliver multiple strategic strikes is an integral part of XPD.

WHO STUDIES XPD?

Without question, XPD is not for everyone. Actually, we find that it is not for most people. Even for those people who want to learn self-defense, XPD is not automatically the right fit. Furthermore, XPD has evolved to encompass a number of levels of proficiency (see below).

XPD was originally designed for the pre-teens and teens of wealthy families. The objective was to enable these young adults to defend themselves so they can escape dangerous situations. Having seen the benefit to their children, some wealthy parents became interested in learning a few highly effective, easy to implement ways to protect themselves as well. This led to the official development of XPD. Here students learn core aspects of combat mindfulness, how to use surprise and speed, and a select number of strategic strikes.

XPD is for people who have limited time to learn self-defense and still want to be highly effective, if need be. It's for people who recognize the need to be able to take matters into their own hands when faced by quite dire events. It's not at all a replacement for top-flight close protection personnel and similar security measures. However, for some people XPD can augment these security measures.

BEYOND XPD

Some people after becoming proficient with XPD want more. This demand led to the development of more extensive versions of the program—Advanced XPD and XPD-Blade.

Advanced XPD is broader and considerably more intense than XPD. There are a number of very distinct differences. One of these differences is the inclusion of a small number of select, carefully chosen, fundamental iron palm conditioning techniques. There's also greater emphasis on situations where there are multiple attackers as well as attackers armed with various types of weapons. Let's take a closer look at iron palm.

Iron palm is a combination of conditioning techniques. There are a number of components of preparation such as building the strength of the muscles within the hand, arm, and shoulder. Many practitioners use Dit Da Jow, a Chinese emollient, after training to avoid damage. Learning to let the striking motions flow effortlessly is essential, which also requires becoming proficient in a number of Quigong exercises.

Why do people study iron palm as part of their martial arts training? Because it enables practitioners to deliver devastatingly destructive strikes with their hands. Being able to turn bricks into powder, to make 4-by-4's literally explode into teeny tiny wood chips, to strike a person's body and stop his or her heart while turning internal organs into mush are all possibilities with iron palm.

The complication is the extensive and never-ending training and conditioning that's required to master and maintain iron palm. While some people we've worked with have gone in this direction, very few individuals have the time and commitment to develop iron palm. Nevertheless, in Advanced XPD we incorporate some of the very basic conditioning techniques in order to make the strategic strikes all the more potent.

Our intent is not to have our students' strike with enough concentrated and deadly power to shatter every rib at once. Instead, our aim is to provide them with the ability to be appreciably more effective when using their hands to strike strategically. While we stress the Rule of Three, people who have even a modicum of iron palm conditioning, commonly after striking with their hands don't have the opportunity to hit their attacker again as he (or she) is completely out of commission.

XPD-Blade is close quarter devastation. It's for people who seek to incorporate knife work into their self-defense repertoire. The moment a blade is introduced into the situation, there's going to be blood and, very likely, severe damage to the attacker. Moreover, the conflict will be over extremely quickly.

The same tactical advantages of XPD are present in XPD-Blade—combat mindfulness, surprise and speed, and strategic strikes. However, training in XPD-Blade requires a greater presence of mind as the practitioner must make near nanosecond decisions concerning the level of destruction he or she is going to inflict. With XPD-Blade we developed an extensive hierarchy of strategic strikes from minor cuts to assured death. The severity of the situation and the discerned intent of the attacker will determine how and where an XPD-Blade practitioner will strike.

To effectively deal with most attackers, it's unlikely a person has to go beyond XPD. Moreover, very few students of XPD have the time or the motivation to learn Advanced XPD or XPD-Blade. Let's keep in mind that XPD was developed because people wanted to be capable of defending themselves in severe situations without having to make a major commitment of time. Nevertheless, for those individuals who become enticed by XPD and want more, it only made sense to make "more" available.

CONCLUSION

If your life or the lives of your loved ones were on the line, would you fight back? While most people, if not everyone, would probably say "yes," the question then is, "Can you fight back?" We suspect that the majority, who would want to fight back, lacks the knowledge and skills to do so.

XPD is one possibility for people who want to be able to personally defend themselves and their loved ones when confronted with attackers in situations that are potentially life threatening. For the wealthy, we see XPD as supplementing—never replacing—other security measures such as close protection personnel.

XPD is not magic. It's a particular mind-set exploiting an attacker's overconfidence combined with a limited number of potent strategic strikes. XPD is a systematic battle methodology that can be readily learned over a relatively short period of time. While the range of techniques are carefully selected and few in number, the need for extensive and persistent practice is an absolute requirement in order to commit these techniques to "muscle memory."

For those individuals who find value in XPD and are looking for more, there are two options—Advanced XPD and XPD-Blade. Both require a much higher level of dedication in order to become competent.

George Chaber is an internationally accomplished martial artist and the developer of XPD. He's more renowned as an educator in the field—a teacher of teachers. George is the owner and head instructor of Karate America (www.karateamericabethel.com).

Jerry D. Prince is an adept fighter with multiple black belts. When not practicing how to cripple assailants, he's often creating videos (jdprincestudios.com), hanging out with his friends, or taking care of his bunnies.

CHAPTER 20

THE FAMILY OFFICE
SOLUTION

by Russ Alan Prince, Richard J. Flynn
& Steffianna Claiden

INCREASINGLY, THE EXCEPTIONALLY AFFLUENT

are turning to family offices to address many of their financial and life issues. This trend is prompting many of the traditional providers such as private banks and brokerage firms as well as accounting and law firms to establish their own family office practices for their wealthiest clients. This client-intensive renaissance is a by-product of the conflicting loyalties of some of the professional advisors the very wealthy have hired as well as the sometimes questionable advice they received (*see Chapter 9: Selecting Professional Advisors*).

WHAT ARE FAMILY OFFICES?

Their deep understanding and responsiveness to exceptionally affluent families characterize family offices. With such diversity under the heading of family offices, their offerings can be equally varied, but generally speaking, family offices, writ large, tend to provide two principal categories of services: those that relate to managing wealth and those that relate to family support. Under the umbrella of wealth management, we often find investment management, advanced planning, and private investment banking. Simultaneously, under support services we often see administrative and lifestyle services.

In practice, each of these sub-categories is comprised of specific products (such as private equity funds or intentionally defective trusts) and services (bill paying and close protection personnel, for example) based on the needs of the underlying families. The sheer scope of possibilities and combinations mean that truly unique and thorny issues can be addressed in wholly customized new types of family offices without deviating from the basic operating structure.

Basically, there are two types of family offices based on the number of families involved —single-family offices and multi-family offices. Let's now look at each of them.

The single-family office. Broadly speaking, a single-family office is an organizational structure that manages the financial and personal affairs of one wealthy family. Because a single-family office is driven purely by the needs and preferences of the underlying family, there is no standard for how one should be structured and a variety of models are in use around the globe.

Some single-family offices, for instance, are lean enterprises that focus exclusively on investing with a skeleton crew, while others are robust organizations with in-house staff, numerous vendor relationships, and a broad platform of services. This disparity means it's difficult to establish hard-and-fast criteria for how a single-family office should be defined other than its dedication to a sole family unit. Estimates of the number of single-family offices range from a few thousand to the tens of thousands.

There are seven significant reasons the exceptionally affluent choose to set up single-family offices. Generally, in order of importance they are:

1 **Control.** A dominant characteristic of the individuals who opted to put a single-family office in place is a penchant for control. An exceptionally wealthy family is able to design and set the management parameters— the policies and practices—in place for their single-family office. This results in an organization that delivers highly personalized expertise to the ultra-wealthy family.

Greater coordination of professional advisors is a usual benefit of the single-family office. The decision-makers inside the single-family office typically choose the outside experts. Selection is based primarily on competence, and that, coupled with powerful incentives to mitigate costs and achieve optimal results, mean the ultra-wealthy family benefits from real synergies and real talents.

All in all, the desire by the ultra-wealthy family to exercise significant control over their financial and personal lives is the core driving force for them to establish single-family offices. What's so very telling is that this motivation powerfully impacts all the other motivations to create a single-family office.

2 **Tight oversight of professional advisors.** As noted (see *Chapter 9: Selecting Professional Advisors*), ensuring that they're not being cheated or exploited is very important to the ultra-wealthy. This requires extensive due diligence when selecting professionals as well as continuous and careful ongoing monitoring of these professionals. The single-family office proves to be an excellent means to maintain a very high level of oversight and supervision.

Combining the anticipated greater use of outside professionals (see below) with the need for control and wanting to maximize the value to the family of these professionals, the importance of choosing and managing them is becoming a more fundamental and critical role of single-family offices.

3 **Aligned with the family's agenda.** More and more, many ultra-wealthy families are finding some of the more traditional providers such as private banks, brokerage houses, and the like to be lacking for a variety of reasons. Many of these families have considerable experience working with these providers. However, those experiences are, in part, the motivation to create their single-family offices.

What's also telling is that their ability to access other types of professionals for non-financial services has also proved quite vexing. While the ultra-wealthy families are able to access such expertise, the ability to select the best and then manage them effectively can prove very problematic.

By having a group of professionals working for them and only them, the ultra-wealthy family is making certain that their needs, wants, and preferences are always center stage. This focus on being able to better address the wishes and requirements of the family point directly back to the very strong preference for control these ultra-wealthy families are looking for.

4 **Extreme confidentiality.** The ultra-wealthy seriously value their privacy (see *Chapter 8: Critical Lifestyle Services*). They generally want their personal and professional information kept extremely private.

The single-family office pretty consistently acts as a permeable barrier between the family and specified people and institutions. There are a variety of ways directly and through proxies, forthright and crafty, that the single-family office is able to ensure the privacy of the ultra-wealthy family.

5 **Expanded access to business opportunities.** The ability to leverage the family's wealth, relationships, expertise, and stature can be amplified by a single-family office. While often requiring a very proactive networking strategy (see *Chapter 14: Street-Smart Networking*), the end results can prove to be amazing.

This is exemplified when a momentously broader spectrum of high-caliber business opportunities come their way. Seeking out extremely high-quality "club deals," for example, is increasingly a focus among single-family offices, and they're anticipated to figure more prominently in the portfolio of these boutiques over the next five years, which parallels the interest ultra-wealthy inheritors have in such direct investments (see *Chapter 7: Doing Deals*).

6 **Educate family members.** For many, the single-family office is considered a means to help educate family members on a variety of issues and concerns as well as the operations and philosophy of the family. The educational function of the single-family office is rapidly undergoing a transformation with respect to the methodologies employed as well as the topics covered (see *Chapter 11: The Education of Global Stewards*). Along with family security and concierge healthcare (see *Chapter 8: Critical Lifestyle Services*), education will become a leading support service provided by single-family offices.

7 **Achieve economies of scale.** A major industry advantage of the single-family office is the aggregation of their wealth under a cooperative arrangement. When deftly addressed, this provides considerable leverage internally and with outside professionals. The consequence is obtaining greater results while mitigating costs.

Irrespective of wealth, single-family offices are certainly not for everyone. The first cousin to the single-family office is the multi-family office.

The multi-family office. Conceptually, the multi-family office structure is an extension of the current ubiquitous wealth management model: a business helping firms engage in fewer, deeper, and more lasting relationships with affluent clients based on customized solutions, specialized expertise, and responsive service. In reality, however, many kinds of entities identify themselves as multi-family offices creating an expansive field of disparate contenders.

Though today's multi-family offices often come from dissimilar backgrounds—some were single-family offices looking to share infrastructure costs, others were small groups of like-minded families who saw an opportunity to expand, and still others were commercial entities that chose to focus narrowly on the needs of the ultra-wealthy—they're now organizations with common attributes and are run with an eye toward profit and growth. In fact, multi-family offices are businesses where the primary motivation is to make a profit. This doesn't negate their potential intense commitment to serving their ultra-wealthy clients, but in contrast to single-family offices, profit tops their needs hierarchy.

While multi-family offices are commercial enterprises, the good ones are as focused on deftly serving their ultra-wealthy family clients as are the professionals hired into a single-family office. Moreover, they usually offer the core sets of expertise that most single-family offices provide. The complication is to discern the true high-caliber multi-family offices from the pretenders.

FOUR KEY TRENDS

While the inherent confusion surrounding defining what is a family office makes trend analysis challenging, there are, nevertheless, four very powerful and pervasive trends impacting the industry, writ large. One trend affects both single and multi-family offices. We're seeing considerable growth in strategic outsourcing. Another trend is limited to multi-family offices. It's the establishment of multi-family offices with particular niche expertise. The third trend is the transitioning of the compensation packages to an increasingly participatory model usually inherent in multi-family offices, but it is catching fire in single-family offices. Finally, we see family offices becoming ever more capable in serving their very wealthy clients.

Let's take a closer look at each of these trends.

Strategic outsourcing. Family offices—both single and multi-family offices—are often expensive propositions. They're generally very much boutique businesses employing high-caliber experts for the betterment of the very wealthy.

The costs of running a family office have always been a consideration, but have fallen under even more scrutiny since 2008. Concurrently, the very wealthy have become clearer and more precise on just what expertise they need in various circumstances. Combining these two considerations, we find that the family offices creating the best solutions for the ultra-wealthy are the ones:

1. Identifying and concentrating on their high-impact core capabilities, and

2. Strategically outsourcing non-core capabilities, while

3. Maintaining diligent supervision over all the professionals involved including those delivering the non-core capabilities.

In working with family offices, we find that these three organizational competences can prove problematic. The ability to determine and justify core versus non-core capabilities is often fairly difficult for many wealthy families. Big picture, the following equation conceptually captures the factors that need to be evaluated in determining whether to outsource capabilities:

163

(Frequency + Criticality) − (Cost + Exclusivity) = **DETERMINATION**

- **Frequency** is the likely amount of usage by the family office for the expertise.

- **Criticality** is the importance of the expertise to the family office.

- **Cost** is the differential expense of the expertise depending on whether it's in-house or outsourced.

- **Exclusivity** is the level of requisite proprietary access to the expertise.

- **Determination** is whether to bring the expertise in-house or not.

Another complication of being able to adroitly select professionals to outsource to is fraught with the potential for disaster. This is a function of decreased control thereby making finding independent professionals a very important consideration and process (see *Chapter 9: Selecting Professional Advisors*). While there are all sorts of possible problems with strategic outsourcing, having the entire requisite and desired expertise in-house regularly overshadows them, and this doesn't even take into account the severe adverse cost differential.

Strategic outsourcing, in effect, is an extremely powerful and ubiquitous trend in the family office universe. The issue is to engage in strategic outsourcing wisely. The answer is often extensive and ongoing diagnostic assessments coupled with the structural flexibility to adjust quickly.

Niche multi-family offices. If the decision is to go with a multi-family office, the knowledge base and experience of its key people should be carefully weighed and taken into account. It's very much a truism that all wealthy people are not alike. For example, as noted in *Chapter 1: Ultra-Wealthy Inheritors*, there are commonly distinct and pronounced differences between those who first create great personal fortunes and those who initially inherited great personal fortunes.

While the offerings of many family offices no matter what the orientation remain the same, applications of these sets of expertise can be more or less geared to a particular clientele. Two examples of this are celebrity family offices and outpost family offices.

Through talent and a bit of luck, some entertainers and athletes capture fame and fortune. And like other wealthy individuals, these celebrities have a variety of financial needs from wealth management to support services. While celebrities do have some of the same generic needs as everybody else, what regularly differentiates them are those issues specific to the entertainment and sports businesses. These require specialized knowledge and skills and an intimate understanding of the celebrities in order to achieve optimal results.

Celebrities seeking professionals are increasingly attracted to the multi-family office model, which integrates core aspects of a business manager's job with a broad array of financial and legal specializations. When celebrities call on professionals to develop a business model, for example, it means the professionals must go beyond the role of a traditional multi-family office, beyond the role of a business manager, or even that of a management consultant because they're tackling the wealthy celebrity client's financial and tax issues all along the way. The celebrity client's lifestyle also comes into play.

In this capacity, the celebrity multi-family office is taking on a number of functions simultaneously and seamlessly. What makes it all work so well is the highly integrated nature of the endeavor.

Another multi-family office variation gaining great traction is the outpost family office. This is where a single-family or multi-family office in one geographic region creates a relationship with a multi-family office in another geographic reason. The trend is burgeoning because it's a cost-effective way to provide the highest quality responsiveness and oversight across the world as well as providing on-the-ground supervision of certain types of investments, related activities, and being able to deliver specific specialized capabilities.

Aside from being on call for the wealthy clients or family members of a family office, an expanding role of the outpost family office is the acquisition and oversight on specific types of investments—lately involving real estate and middle-market companies. In these situations, local (which can be countrywide) coverage and "on-the-ground expertise" is required.

The outpost family office is not inherently a new concept. On the contrary, the joint-arrangements between boutique private banks to address the issues noted go back generations. Conceptually, the foreign domiciled family office/outpost family office arrangement is the same as the various worldwide accounting and legal networks enabling professional services firms to address client needs worldwide. While a new business model for family offices, the outpost family office has considerable history and potential.

Participatory compensation arrangements. As with all professional services firms whose success is based on brainpower, family offices need to attract and motivate talented individuals. This has become a very critical matter for single-family offices who, understandably, want to ensure they have extremely capable people at the helm. It's fundamentally less of an issue for multi-family offices due to the for-profit nature of these enterprises. Therefore, we'll discuss the compensation arrangements for key personnel, which are becoming increasingly normative at single-family offices.

It's fair to say that historically the way key personnel were paid at single-family offices was a combination of salary and benefits, plus bonuses. The bonuses were usually highly discretionary, as they weren't tied to specific performance criteria. Instead, family members determined the bonuses based on any number of relevant and irrelevant factors. This approach to compensation still appears to dominate the world of single-family offices. However, the winds are shifting.

With an emphasis by single-family offices of making sure they have high-caliber talent in charge—especially when it comes to investing—there's movement to a compensation arrangement predicated on "sharing." This has resulted in the development of participatory compensation arrangements at single-family offices.

Simply, with participatory compensation arrangements, key personnel at the single-family office have a financial stake in the family office itself (accomplished in various ways) or select investments or both. Participatory compensation arrangements can result in a strong alignment of interests between the key personnel and the very wealthy family being served.

To make participatory compensation arrangements work efficaciously, they have to be well designed and implemented. Unfortunately, this is where we see many single-family offices fall short.

The following is the process we've employed to develop participatory compensation arrangements in single-family offices. This methodology is applicable for all senior personnel at a single-family office and is also very viable for most multi-family offices. It's also important to recognize that—due to the generally idiosyncratic nature of single-family offices—the best compensation arrangements are negotiations aiming for balance. There are a series of steps that the parties transverse in creating the compensation package:

STEP 1 **Determining the parameters.** It's very useful to begin by setting and clearly specifying the constraints that are acceptable to all parties. We find that comparative compensation—while fraught with limitations—proves to be a useful starting point provided reasonable comparisons could be made. At the same time, it's essential to determine where it makes the most sense for both sides to have key personnel participating.

STEP 2 **Structuring the compensation package.** Once there is general agreement on the parameters, it's possible to focus on various ways to implement. This regularly includes evaluating a number of possible legal and related techniques and products. The use of certain kinds of partnerships, for example, has proven to be very viable in that they can be established where monies are provided to key personnel when hurdles are met while also possessing effective claw back capabilities.

STEP 3 **Establishing a contingency plan.** If something unfortunate happens to the family member(s) making the decisions or to the key personnel without a contingency plan, the single-family office can possibly turn into a train wreck. There are two components to a well-conceptualized contingency plan. One is the game plan detailing how responsibilities and roles are transitioned. The other component is financial, often accomplished by the skilled use of trust or corporate structures, sometimes in conjunction for life insurance or sinking funds or equity. Whatever the approach, it's advantageous to tie it tightly with any participatory compensation arrangement.

STEP

4

Refining the compensation package. Even when everyone happily agrees with the compensation package, it often needs to be tweaked over time. Factors not previously considered very important as well as how people believe they will respond but don't, combined with changing agendas, results in compensation packages that require adjustments.

Increasing proficiency of family offices. The competition for the business of the exceptionally affluent is actually multiplying faster than the exceptionally affluent are multiplying. This is not surprising considering these professional advisors can profit handsomely by delivering world-class expertise to these individuals. Competition among these professional advisors is proving very beneficial for the ultra-wealthy. It's raising the bar so that the family offices are more competent than ever, and this scenario is likely to only intensify.

The level of expertise and responsiveness needs to be at the very top end of the scale because the ultra-wealthy have options. It's not just that they have options, but they're making a concerted effort to evaluate them ongoing and are, more than ever, willing to make changes expeditiously. This is the case as they evaluate the performance of the multi-family office they're using or the personnel of their own single-family office.

The competencies of family offices are going up, in part, because of strategic outsourcing (see above). The ability to seek out and readily exchange professionals enables family offices to constantly work to ensure the "best" experts are engaged. This is resulting in a much more intense approach to sourcing outside professionals (see *Chapter 9: Selecting Professional Advisors*). In some situations, such as with various advanced planning strategies (see *Chapter 6: Wealth Management*), competition is making it easy to receive second, and sometimes third, opinions. This risk mitigation strategy works to give the ultra-wealthy a better understanding of the possibilities that are available to them.

Family offices are looking to hire professionals—internally or on an outsourced basis—who are more than industry thought leaders. For the professionals who want to work with the very well-to-do, it's progressively not enough to do what they do (even) amazingly well, be at the cutting-edge of their profession, and contribute to its advancement. Becoming "knowledge entrepreneurs" is fast becoming a criteria to be engaged (see *Chapter 9: Selecting Professional Advisors*). The ultra-wealthy use of knowledge entrepreneurs translates into them obtaining meaningfully superior solutions.

The levels of comprehension the ultra-wealthy are expecting from the professional advisors they employ cover two partially overlapping areas. They want the experts they engage to be outstanding experts. That is, they want them to be amazingly erudite and competent when it comes to the field of specialization, whether it's life insurance (see *Chapter 16: Sophisticated Advanced Planning Using Life Insurance*) or personal defense (see *Chapter 19: Taking Matters Into Their Own Hands*) or whatever the matter.

At the same time, professionals, no matter how adept they are, will not be successful with the ultra-wealthy unless they have a detailed in-depth understanding of their world. It's these insights coupled with state-of-the-art know-how that produce desired customized and often sophisticated solutions.

In sum, due to competitive pressures combined with a more and more astute clientele—the ultra-wealthy—family offices are constantly exploring new ways to add exponential value. This translates into them becoming increasingly proficient.

CONCLUSION

The ultra-wealthy are increasingly finding the family office to be the solution to their various financial and lifestyle concerns. Whether it's a single-family office or a multi-family office, the intense focus on addressing a range of preferences, needs, and wants in a holistic manner is quite appealing to them. Thus, we expect many ultra-wealthy inheritors who are presently without a family office relationship to seriously consider establishing their own single-family office or availing themselves of the services and capabilities of a multi-family office.

In considering using a family office, it's important to understand how the industry is changing. The trends we described—strategic outsourcing, niche multi-family offices, and participatory compensation agreements for key personnel in single-family offices—need to be taken into account in order to make the best decision concerning which direction to take.

Another trend also quite important to note is that the bar will continue to rise. That is, the quality of family offices is going to—in fits and starts—significantly improve. This is a function of the greater demands and requirements of the ultra-wealthy coupled with an ever more motivated and qualified array of professional advisors seeking to work with them.

Steffianna Claiden is founder and CEO of Family Office Review *and* Family Office Capital Network. *Family Office Review (www.familyofficereview.com) is an online magazine-style publication providing information on financial and life management issues to high net worth individuals, family businesses, entrepreneurs, and family offices around the world. Family Office Capital Network (www.focapnet.com) offers educational information and events on private direct deals, intra-family co-investing, private equity, and alternative asset class investing.*

CODA

SEVEN TRENDS CHANGING THE WORLD OF ULTRA-WEALTHY INHERITORS

THE DRAWBACK TO PREDICTING the future is a certainty of being wrong, at least to some degree. A lot of this prognostication is based on basically straight-line projections. These linear-oriented forecasts are highly susceptible to disruptive and unanticipated influences from technology to major societal shifts proving our projections inaccurate. Hence, we graciously admit our crystal ball is cracked.

With this disclaimer soundly in place, we nevertheless see a number of very pronounced trends that will influence the world of ultra-wealthy inheritors. What's important to recognize is that these trends are very likely to ripple through society in various impactful ways. For example, their prominent focus on outcome-driven philanthropy will certainly have a bearing on the non-profit sector. This perspective will likely push some charitable organizations to operate differently—hopefully more efficaciously. It will also likely change the prevailing zeitgeist for major and planned giving.

There's no question of the trickle down effect where the wealthy start the ball moving. An example of this is concierge medicine (see *Chapter 8: Critical Lifestyle Services; Chapter 17: Connected Care for the High-Net-Worth Family: Millennials Will Lead the Way*). Here the wealthy are financing a changing healthcare delivery model creating new best practices. These new best practices are being codified enabling them to migrate to the broad population.

We've identified seven powerful interconnected trends affecting the world of ultra-wealthy inheritors over the next few years:

- The growth of a cohort.

- Ultra-wealthy inheritors will take the reins.

- Ultra-wealthy inheritors will work to significantly enhance and refine their knowledge and capabilities.

- Ultra-wealthy inheritors will increasingly focus on outcome driven philanthropy.

- Ultra-wealthy inheritors will increasingly make private deals a focus of their wealth creating activities.

- Ultra-wealthy inheritors will be actively involved in the selecting and overseeing of professional advisors.

- Many ultra-wealthy inheritors will embrace global stewardship.

Let's now briefly consider each of these trends.

THE GROWTH OF A COHORT

Relatively speaking, great wealth is multiplying in numbers of people and even more in the size of their fortunes. It's very evident that the ultra-wealthy are capitalizing on globalization, technology, and expanding professional sophistication to amass ever-greater wealth.

There will also be a boon in significant wealth creation over the decade. New technologies, the application of superior business processes and people result in them building great fortunes. The probability of this happening is greater than most any time in history. These fortunes will transfer down the line. So, the number of ultra-wealthy inheritors will continue to expand.

At the same time, there's a worldwide demographic shift whereby the children, grandchildren, and those further down the line of extreme wealth creators will be inheriting significant monies. These heirs are being provided with considerable and sometimes astounding fortunes. Moreover, it's evident that this transitioning of exceptional riches is likely to accelerate throughout this decade.

This growth in ultra-wealthy inheritors will have many societal repercussions. Two exceptionally positive consequences are their likely commitment to entrepreneurial capitalism and their strong motivation to change the world in momentous ways (see *Chapter 2: Inheriting More Than Money*; *Chapter 3: With Great Wealth Comes Great Responsibility*). The key to all this will be their success at harnessing and applying their array of personal, family, and professional resources.

ULTRA-WEALTHY INHERITORS WILL TAKE THE REINS

In many ways from creating their own business empires to working to make a resounding philanthropic impact, ultra-wealthy inheritors are on the march. For some it will be a means to come out of the family's shadow. For many, it's the way they will actualize their own ambitions and dreams.

It's very clear in the research as well as in our experience working with ultra-wealthy inheritors that they're generally very focused in taking control over their wealth and their lives. Without question, they're taking the reins.

An area where this is playing out in a pronounced way is where ultra-wealthy inheritors will take charge of the determination and relationships with the professional advisors they choose to employ (see below). Very clearly, they'll be active participants in the way their monies are deployed. Moreover, they'll be ever more increasingly looking for quantifiable as well as qualified results of their decisions.

Part of them taking the reins entails a more constructive and proactive approach to working with other ultra-wealthy families including their peers. Recognizing kindred spirits, many ultra-wealthy inheritors are inclined to align themselves with individuals with similar orientations and perspectives (see *Chapter 5: Philanthropy*; *Chapter 7: Doing Deals*). The key is to learn to most efficaciously and powerfully use their extensive networks (see *Chapter 13: Bargaining Brilliance*; *Chapter 14: Street-Smart Networking*).

ULTRA-WEALTHY INHERITORS WILL WORK TO SIGNIFICANTLY ENHANCE AND REFINE THEIR KNOWLEDGE AND CAPABILITIES

While there will always be parasitic "trust babies," a large percentage of ultra-wealthy inheritors will be driven to make a difference in creative and personal ways. They'll look to do so across many aspects of their lives such as dealing with the financial facets of their inheritances and their charitable endeavors. Many ultra-wealthy inheritors are inclined to become global stewards (see below).

What's quite telling is that in order to actualize their personal and professional agendas, a percentage of them will need to learn and develop or upgrade their abilities. Growing up in the families they did often provides insights if not lessons (see *Chapter 2: Inheriting More than Money*) that produce success. Coupled with their own acumen, personal integrity, and self-reflective honesty, many ultra-wealthy inheritors substitute self-delusion for a strong desire for self-development.

As noted (see *Chapter 4: Enhancing Expertise*), ultra-wealthy inheritors recognize certain areas where further expertise is important. In particular, negotiating proficiencies and the ability to make really powerful use of their extensive and influential networks top the list (see *Chapter 13: Bargaining Brilliance; Chapter 14: Street-Smart Networking*). Additionally, a number of them are inclined to become more technically expert.

Ultra-wealthy inheritors will use a variety of edifying forums and methods to become more informed and capable. Engaging peers will likely play a solid role (see *Chapter 10: Helping Wealthy Inheritors Change the World*), so too are formal "courses" as well as various education-on-demand modalities (see *Chapter 11: The Education of Global Stewards*). At the same time, their informal education—the experience of working with leading experts in various fields—will play a major role in their advancement.

ULTRA-WEALTHY INHERITORS WILL INCREASINGLY FOCUS ON OUTCOME-DRIVEN PHILANTHROPY

It's evident that many ultra-wealthy inheritors want to use their financial, personal, and family resources to have a meaningful positive impact on the world (see *Chapter 5: Philanthropy; Chapter 10: Helping Wealthy Inheritors Change the World*). As with many aspects of their lives, they're taking a hands-on approach. It's decreasingly a matter of just writing a check.

Because these ultra-wealthy inheritors want to make a meaningful difference, they're looking for outcome-driven results. Good intentions and trying hard are vanishing as sole "legitimate" justifications for charitable causes to receive their largess. They are increasingly focused on getting meaningful results from their philanthropic efforts.

Their desire for making a significant difference will ofttimes translate into working with their peers as well as institutions to synergize and leverage resources. In soliciting commitment from others, or adding to someone else's charitable activities, the need to be results-focused becomes a greater imperative.

ULTRA-WEALTHY INHERITORS WILL INCREASINGLY FOCUS THEIR WEALTH CREATING ACTIVITIES ON PRIVATE DEALS

The attraction of private deals including club deals to enhance their personal fortunes will only intensify (see *Chapter 7: Doing Deals*). While this focus in no way eliminates the use of professional advisors to manage portions of their overall investment portfolio, for ultra-wealthy inheritors interested in creating new wealth, their personal attention will more and more be on sourcing high-potential deals. Some of them will also be heavily involved in moving those deals to completion.

When it comes to deal making, the ultra-wealthy inheritors will be involved in—broadly speaking—any of three ways. One is "industry knowledge." This is often a function of the way the family built their fortunes. Then there are technical proficiencies. This has a lot to do with the mechanics of putting the deal together and is unlikely to be core for many ultra-wealthy inheritors. Also, there are process proficiencies such as negotiating skills, which have been noted to be an area many ultra-wealthy inheritors are looking to improve upon (see above).

The ultra-wealthy inheritors can also provide capital out of their own pockets and by tapping their network (see *Chapter 14: Street-Smart Networking*). The third contribution they can make is by bringing a deal to the table. As ultra-wealthy inheritors become more adept at managing and artfully growing their networks, they'll prove increasingly capable of sourcing both capital and deals.

ULTRA-WEALTHY INHERITORS WILL BE ACTIVELY INVOLVED IN THE SELECTION AND OVERSEEING OF PROFESSIONAL ADVISORS

The growth of the cohort (see above) will be matched by the growth in the number of professional advisors seeking to do business with them. With the greater involvement of the ultra-wealthy inheritors in choosing (see *Chapter 9: Selecting Professional Advisors*) and monitoring professional advisors, many of them will not meet the higher and higher standards this cohort will be setting.

The days of coupon-clipping inheritors are long, long...long gone. From deceptions to mismanagements to a lack of professionalism, ultra-wealthy inheritors are generally very circumspect concerning the professionals they employ. Consequently, they will take ardent control over this aspect of their lives. The "trust me" approach invoked by many professional advisors will not at all be acceptable. It will be soundly replaced by a "prove it to me" approach adopted by the ultra-wealthy inheritors.

The establishment of single-family offices as well as other mechanisms to obtain a more coordinated management of their financial and personal affairs—where they're in control—is expected (see *Chapter 20: The Family Office Solution*). It's not only their money that's at stake, but their personal and family security and health that will be addressed by these coordinating operations.

MANY ULTRA-WEALTHY INHERITORS WILL EMBRACE GLOBAL STEWARDSHIP

It's highly questionable if the current direction and approach to global development is sustainable. If this is the case, then there's the guarantee of widespread interconnected societal, economic, and environmental small and large disasters. A norm of instability supported by continuous calamities will only intensify competition and conflicts throughout the world.

Across the board there's a strong movement toward global stewardship. It's all about asking and answering the question, "What kind of world do you want to live in?" We've concluded that a disproportion of ultra-wealthy inheritors are asking this question and, consequently, are looking for solutions to address a fragile and problem-ridden world.

Ultra-wealthy inheritors for a plethora of reasons are exceedingly well positioned to take on the mantel of global stewards. From their transnational worldview to the wealth they influence (see *Chapter 1: Ultra-Wealthy Inheritors*) coupled with practical reasoning, with an ofttimes self-reflective nature and considerable integrity, ultra-wealthy inheritors can and will make excellent global stewards. Furthermore, as many of them are committed to life-long learning, there are many opportunities for them to refine and enhance their knowledge and skills (see *Chapter 4: Enhancing Expertise*; *Chapter 11: The Education of Global Stewards*).

Because of their desire to improve and their motivation to achieve, because of the way they're seeking to establish themselves in the world, ultra-wealthy inheritors are forcefully taking the reins of their lives and their inheritances. Many of them will have a very positive transformative impact on the world we all share.

APPENDIX

LIMITATIONS
WHEN RESEARCHING
WEALTH

FOR MORE THAN A QUARTER CENTURY, we have been
studying private wealth. We've dissected the mind-set and behaviors of the wealthy
to discern best practices. We've evaluated their determination and use of professional
advisors including the subsequent effectiveness of these experts. We've analyzed
the philanthropic behavior of the wealthy addressing preferences and efficacy.
With all these research studies to our credit, we believe that the cumulative
aggregation of this knowledge over time provides an increasingly clear understanding
of a remarkably obscure universe.

The world of the wealthy—especially the ultra-wealthy—is often veiled, if not out
and out purposely opaque. There are a multitude of reasons for this, not the
least of which is to ensure their own safety and the safety of their loved ones
(see *Chapter 8: Critical Lifestyle Services*). Hence, motivating them to fill out
surveys can quite problematic.

At the same time, a bane of all survey research as well as many other types of research is the veracity of the respondents. For all sorts of reasons, the wealthy might embellish the truth. It's not uncommon to confront self-enhancement biases among research participants. Nevertheless, there are methodologies that can be employed to gain the understandings and insights we're looking for. For example, whenever possible we look for multiple confirmations of the outcomes of situations and try not to rely exclusively on single responses from the research participants. Unfortunately, many times all we have is what the wealthy survey respondent reported, and consequently, that's what we report.

What habitually proves to be the most challenging and complicated part of researching the wealthy is sampling. A central problem to researching meaningful wealth in any context, including ultra-wealthy inheritors, is gaining access to interested and knowledgeable participants. All such research involves purposeful samples. Moreover, chain-referral sampling is a requisite when studying the wealthy and often those in their service.

The use of chain-referral sampling does indeed bias the results as it constrains the set of potential respondents. For example, considering the criteria we set for inclusion (see *Chapter 1: Ultra-Wealthy Inheritors*), while we're comfortable with the floor we set concerning the size of the family fortune, we were rarely able to independently verify the level of influence the survey respondents have over these assets.

As noted in *Chapter 3: With Great Wealth Comes Great Responsibility*, the ultra-wealthy inheritors who comprise this research study are, by and large, motivated to constructively change the world. They are generally interested in philanthropy and impact investing (see *Chapter 5: Philanthropy*; *Chapter 6: Wealth Management*). We're well aware that there are ultra-wealthy inheritors who are only interested in amassing greater wealth having no philanthropic interests whatsoever.

Without question, chain-referral sampling can diminish the generalizability of the findings. However, to our knowledge, there's no other viable alternative to gather quantitative data on the wealthy, and this is even more the case when it comes to the ultra-wealthy.

Another consideration—because of the relative scarcity of the total population of ultra-wealthy inheritors—is the small sample size of our study. There are two issues here. One is that we don't know the size of the potential universe. That is, we don't know, nor do we believe anyone with any degree of real accuracy can tell us how many ultra-wealthy inheritors—by our definition—there are in the world. This again talks to the restrictions in generalizing the results.

Because we were only able to survey 144 ultra-wealthy inheritors, the generalizability of these findings is highly questionable. This is a given with respect to all the research we conduct with the wealthy. It's unavoidable.

To derive a more expansive and telling understanding of the exceptionally affluent, whenever possible, we engage in ethnographic research. Technically put: the aim of ethnography is to study selected members of a society in their natural environments and produce detailed case analyses explaining key aspects of their behaviors and the results of those behaviors.

The way to predominantly collect the data with respect to ultra-wealthy inheritors is through participant observation and interviews. A high degree of precision, being ephetic and ensuring discretion—especially discretion—are essential attributes of anyone wanting to conduct ethnographic research with the wealthy and ultra-wealthy.

There are serious complications when conducting ethnographic research with the wealthy. The ability to be truly objective in our assessments is one such complication. For example, when engaging in activities with the wealthy, it's often quite difficult to remain clinically detached. In interviewing them, as with surveys, a very powerful complication is due to the self-enhancement bias. All told, ethnographic research with the wealthy is regularly fraught with minor and major tribulations.

The following table (Exhibit) highlights the difficulty in researching the wealthy. Understanding these difficulties and weaknesses is essential when considering the research results.

EXHIBIT Limitations When Researching the Wealthy

LIMITATION	IMPLICATION EXAMPLE
Purposely opaque universe	Getting respondents is very difficult
Self-enhancement biases	Veracity of responses
Chain-referral sampling	Limits potential respondents
Unknown size of universe	Impossible to obtain a random sample
Small sample size	Selection bias
Participant observation	Ability to be objective is difficult

What all this means is that the findings of this and all similar types of studies have to be carefully considered when conceptualizing the thought processes and actions of the ultra-wealthy. The research results have to be thought through any time someone extrapolates the findings to other members of this cohort as defined. Consequently, we readily recognize and admit the weaknesses in the research. We want to make clear that the findings are only directional, and they can provide a working foundation to take constructive action.

ABOUT THE AUTHORS

RUSS ALAN PRINCE

Russ Alan Prince is president of
R.A. Prince & Associates, Inc.
He consults with the ultra-wealthy
and professionals to strategically
expand their networks and maximize
the value of their relationships. He is
co-founder and executive director of
Private Wealth magazine.

www.russalanprince.com
www.pw-mag.com

JARED DUBEY

Jared Dubey is an advisor for a global
wealth management firm. He advises
family offices, their beneficial owners and
heirs on matters of asset management
and structuring, philanthropy and impact
investing and intergenerational wealth
transfer and family governance.
Prior to his current role, he worked
for a Single-Family Office based in
the U.S. and Monaco. He currently
lives in New York City.

RICHARD J. FLYNN

Rick Flynn is managing partner
at Flynn Family Office Solutions,
a multi-family office serving the world's
wealthiest families and their advisors.
An international authority on family
offices, he works with clients including
entrepreneurs, athletes, artists,
entertainers, business owners,
executives, and asset managers to
create wealth management strategies
that encompass both lifestyle
management and financial objectives.

www.flynnfamilyoffice.com

BRETT VAN BORTEL

Brett Van Bortel is a Director of
Consulting Services for a major
asset manager. He is responsible for
developing some of the industry's most
highly regarded high-net-worth client
acquisition and retention strategies,
and delivers speeches and coaching
services on these subjects.
He resides in the Chicago suburbs
with his wife and children, and enjoys
athletic pursuits with his children.

ABOUT PRIVATE WEALTH

Private Wealth: Advising the Exceptionally Affluent is for professionals and providers focused on meeting the financial, legal, and lifestyle demands of the ultra-wealthy. This cohort of the affluent collectively wield the greatest purchasing power in the world and, as a result, is the most desirable prospect of financial and legal professionals, luxury brands, and other elite service providers.

Private Wealth delivers thought leadership to the professional and provider by delivering cutting-edge news and research on the ultra-wealthy, the competition, the latest financial and legal strategies, and key lifestyle issues. Additionally, the magazine addresses the insights, processes, and techniques that translate into a successful business focused on the rich and super-rich.

www.pw-mag.com

STREET-SMART NETWORKING

"The step-by-step approach described in this book will unlock a treasure trove of new business for those who have the good sense to implement it. The authors' insights on how to develop and leverage relationships are second to none. "

LEWIS SCHIFF
Author of the highly acclaimed *Business Brilliant* and Executive Director, Inc. Business Owners Council

To order, visit:
www.russalanprince.com

RUSS ALAN PRINCE
BRETT VAN BORTEL